CW00820764

The
Gospel of the Hereafter

By

J. PATERSON-SMYTH, B. D., LL. D., Litt. D., D. C. L.

*Rector of St. Georges, Montreal, Late Professor
of Pastoral Theology, University of Dublin
Author of " How We Got Our Bible," " The
Old Documents and the New Bible," etc., etc., etc.*

NEW YORK   CHICAGO   TORONTO

Fleming   H.   Revell   Company

LONDON   AND   EDINBURGH

New York: 158 Fifth Avenue
Chicago: 17 North Wabash Ave.
London: 21 Paternoster Square
Edinburgh: 75 Princes Street

To My Wife

Contents

Publishers' Note

THIS tenth American (and sixteenth British) edition has been carefully revised and where necessary rewritten by the author. We call special attention to an interesting note on page 108.

This year a Norwegian edition has been published, translated by Judge Hambro of the Supreme Court of Norway assisted by the Bishops of Christiania and Trondheim. Also request has been received for permission to translate the book for readers in Holland. But more interesting is a letter from a Brahmin gentleman in India asking permission to produce at his own cost an edition for his people and dedicated on the front page, " To MY SON, SEREM ALI, WHO IS NOW IN THE NEAR HEREAFTER."

Foreword

THE Lord is risen, but the people do not know it. There is no death, but the people do not believe it. Human life is the most exciting romantic adventure in the Universe, going on stage after stage till we are older than Methuselah and then on again through the infinite eternities—and yet men pass into the Unseen as stupidly as the caterpillar on the cabbage-leaf, without curiosity or joy or wonder or excitement at the boundless career ahead.

Instead of the thrill of coming adventure we have the dull grey monotony of aged lives drawing near the close, and the horror of this war is doubled and the torture of wife or mother as the beloved one crosses the barrier.

What is the matter with us, Christian people? Do we not know? Or have we lost our beliefs? or has imagination grown dulled by too frequent repetition of God's good news?

．　　．　　．　　．

It was so different in early days when the

1

world was younger, when Christ's revelation
was fresh.   Look at St. John, four-score years
and ten, like an eager boy looking into the
Great Adventure : " Beloved, now are we the
sons of God, and IT DOTH NOT YET APPEAR
WHAT WE SHALL BE." [1]

What we shall be !   What we shall be !   Is
not that the chief delight of being young ?
Guessing and hoping and wondering what we
shall be.

The dreariest thing in life is dulness—monotony.   The brightest thing in life is outlook
—vision.   And God has given us that.   Like
St. John we too can stand on the rim of the
world and look out over the wall.

.   .   .   .   .

Life is full of latent possibilities—of outlook,
of romance, of exciting futures.   God has made
it so, if we would only see it.   God's world of
nature has its continuous progress, its ever new
and fascinating stages.   God's caterpillars in
their next stage are going to be soaring butter-
flies—God's acorns are to become mighty oaks
—God's dry little seeds in the granary to-day
will in autumn be alive in the waving harvests.

[1] John iii. 2.

God's world of nature is full of romantic possibilities.

. . . . .

And God's world of men is infinitely more so, and one of life's delights is to know it and look forward to it guessing what we shall be. Outlook. Vision. That is what gives zest to life. That is what we need to make life bright and beautiful.

. . . . .

I see a group of small boys sitting at their play, and their eyes are bright looking into the future. They are going to be soldiers, and sailors, and circus riders, and travelers, and all sorts of things. Because they are boys with the enthusiasms of boyhood, they may be anything. All the possibilities of boyhood belong to them. It doth not yet appear what they shall be, but it is delightful to look forward and speculate about it.

. . . . .

I see them again a dozen years later. They are starting in life, just left college, young soldiers and lawyers and curates and business men—still with their visions and dreams of the future. It doth not yet appear what they shall be, but because they are young men, all that belongs to young manhood lies before them, as they look forward in their day-dreams. What countries they shall live in and what girl they shall marry, and what positions and what work, and what excitements, and what pleasure lie before them. Ah, it is delightful to be young, realizing the possibilities in front— dreaming of what we shall be.

． ． ． ． ．

I see a crowd of older people, men and women dull, uninterested. " We are no longer young," they say, " we are middle-aged or elderly. And we have ceased looking forward. We have lost the vision. We have not become as great as we expected, or as good as we expected. We are fairly comfortable. We have not much to complain of. But life is a bit dull. The path is a bit monotonous now. We have traversed most of it. We can see to the end. There are no more romantic possibilities to make life exciting, no more visions of ' what we shall be.' "

． ． ． ． ．

Don't believe it ! Not a word of it. The

visions are there all right. Look out over the wall. This life of yours is only one of the stages in your career, and not the first stage, either. The first came to you, silent, unconscious, " where the bones do grow in the womb of her that is with child." There you grew and developed for the next move forward. One day came the crisis of birth and you passed into the second stage, the training stage for life and for God. Then through a new crisis you pass on again to new adventures. For God has revealed that what you call death, the end of this career, is but birth into a new and more wondrous career which again passes you forward into still nobler adventures, and that again, perhaps—who knows? Who shall fix the limit?

.   .   .   .   .

Nay, you are not elderly. You are not middle-aged. These are but comparative terms. A house-fly is elderly in twenty-four hours. An oak-tree is young after a hundred years. And you, children of eternity with ages and millenniums before you—you are not even one year old babies in the light of your great future.

Now do you see why the old apostle of Ephesus did not feel aged or elderly—why he looked out like an eager boy into the adventure before him ? "Beloved, now are we the sons of God but we don't know yet what we shall be." Aye, we don't know yet. No more than did the small boys laughing in their play and going to be soldiers and sailors and wonderful people. We don't know yet. But it is all before us. And it is all going to be good because it is in the Father's presence.

So I bid you do what I sometimes do myself, look out into the void and guess like the children what you shall be when you are older than Methuselah.

Shake off the dulness and monotony from your life. Don't talk as if old or middle-aged any more. Be children again in the presence of the Father, and with happy child hearts keep guessing what you shall be.

.   .   .   .   .

I see a woman with the deep pain in her eyes, one of the many mothers whom I have met in these terrible four years. . . . They were afraid to tell her when the War Office telegram came. . . . He had crept out in the night to bring in a wounded chum, and the German sniper got him. At first she could not believe it. It must be some mistake,—some one of similar name. But the days passed on. And the light died in her eyes and she became suddenly old. Her prayers ceased. God had disappointed her. There was nothing left to pray for now. Nothing to be ambitious for any more. Her boy was dead—buried in a shallow grave in France with a little wooden cross at his head. And he was only twenty-two !

.　　　.　　　.　　　.　　　.

The awful waste of it ! All her loving thought over his childhood—all her care, her anxiety, her efforts, her prayers that God would make him a good and noble man. All her hope and pride in the high promise of his boyhood. He was dead. All that he might have been and done in the world was lost. Her life was forever desolate. And God had let it happen !

Kindly friends came to comfort and sympathise. But it was of little use. They had not lost their boy. They could not understand. They bade her be proud that he had died in a noble cause—that he had died to save another. They told her that time would bring a blessed easing to her pain. They told her she must bow to God's mysterious will.

Ah! what is the use of it? How can any outsider intermeddle in the pain of a mother whose boy has just been killed?

> Not all the talking since Adam
> Can make death to be other than death.

.   .   .   .   .

God help us all if there were no better comfort for a tortured world in this hour of its bitterest need—to "make death to be other than death."

.   .   .   .   .

She was a brave woman. She faced the issue clearly. She talked with wise friends. She came back to her prayers. She recalled and relearned the teaching of her Bible and her church which had lain hazily in memory till her need arose. And gradually God's blessed comfort came to her "as to one whom his mother comforteth." Slowly peace came to her heart, and in spite of her pain life became worth living again. . . . He was a good boy. He loved his God. He loved his mother. He had his faults, but she could trust Christ with them. She had had high ambitions for him. Her ambitions came back.

She learned to think of him in the wondrous new adventure, living a full conscious life, thinking and remembering, growing and becoming fitted for the eternal Heaven that is still in front. She believed that the high promise of his boyhood might be fulfilled after all, and that she might one day see it.

Life is still very desolate without him; but she believes that he lives and knows, that he is growing and going on—that he remembers her and loves her as never before, that he is waiting for her, perhaps watching over her as in his days on earth, even though he cannot write home. And trustfully, gratefully she remembers him in her prayers. She thinks that the Heavenly Father is not likely to forget what a mother says to Him about her son.

.   .   .   .   .

This book is a poor, imperfect attempt to put together some of the teachings of our holy religion, to help a troubled world, in this day of its necessity, " to look out over the wall."

PART I

The Near Hereafter

CHAPTER I

"I"

THE title of this chapter is a very short one. It consists of but a single word, and that the shortest word in the whole English language. And though it is the shortest word, yet it is the most wonderful and mysterious word. Though it is a word that every one of us has on his lips every moment of the day, yet no one who reads this book— no one in the whole world—has ever been able to understand what it means.

Just the letter "I."—All day long, from morning till night, we are using it :—I did this. I mean to do that. I ought. I shall. I will. I think. I wish. I love. I hate. I remember. I forget. And so on and on—ever ringing the changes on this little word in all its cases "I" and "my" and "mine" and "me." I want to set you thinking. Who or what is this "I," this "me"?

Perhaps you will say, "Oh, there is nothing mysterious about it—I know very well what I mean by it. 'I' means myself."

But what do I mean by Myself? Of course there is a rough work-day meaning in which it means my whole being as I stand—clothes, body, brains, thoughts, feelings, general appearance, everything. But every thinking man knows that this is not the real "I," that when he says I can, I do, I will, I ought, I remember, the "I" means to him something much deeper and more mysterious than that. Ask yourself, each one, what do you mean by "I"?

§1

Is It My Body? Nay, surely not. I know that my body is only my outward garment woven by "me" out of certain chemical substances. In a scientific museum I can stand before a glass case and see neatly labelled the exact portions of lime and silica and iron and water and other elements which compose my body. I know that this body is continually changing its substance like the rainbow in the sky, like the eddy round a stone in the river. The body I have to-day is no more the body of last year than the fire on my hearth to-night is the fire that was there this morning. I have had a dozen different bodies since I was born, but I am the same still. Every thinking man knows that the " I," the real self, stands behind the body looking out through the windows of the eyes, receiving messages through the portals of the ears. It rules the body, it possesses the body. It says, " I have a body." " This body is a thing belonging to me."

As you watch the changing expression in the face of your friend, as you see his eyes flashing in anger, or softening in affectionate sympathy, do you not feel that all you see is but the outward casing, that the real self of your friend is a something dwelling within?

I hope I am not puzzling you. What I want to do is to introduce you to your own self, to make you really acquainted with that mysterious being in his first stage of existence here and then to follow him out into the great adventure of the Hereafter.

§ 2

Let us go on. What is this I, this self? Is IT MY BRAIN? Physiologists tell us wonderful things of that brain; how its size and shape, and the amount of gray matter modify my character; how it excites itself when I am thinking; how it has different departments for different functions; how it rules and directs everything I do. And men impressed by these wonders have sometimes asserted that there is nothing more to be found. It is the brain which originates all, thought is only certain activities of the brain—memory is only impressions on the substance of the brain—when the brain decays there is no self remaining. What I call "I" is merely a function of my brain.

But immediately the question arises, Which brain? The particles of my brain are always changing. I have had a dozen different brains in my lifetime, with not a particle remaining the same. Which of these brains is it that "I" am only a function of? And how does it happen that I remember what I thought and did and said with the old vanished brains of twenty and thirty years ago? Memory insists that I am still the same "I" in spite of all those changes of brain. If memory be but a series of impressions registered on the brain these could no more survive the dissolution of the brain than impressions on wax could survive the melting of the wax.

Surely my memory, my irresistible conviction of personal identity with my past makes it abundantly clear that " I " am a mysterious unchanging spiritual being behind this ever changing brain.

And that is what the best modern science asserts—that the brain is but my instrument. If we compare it to a violin then " I " am the unseen violin player behind it. The musician cannot produce violin music without a violin, but also the violin cannot produce a musical note, much less take part in a complex symphony without the musician behind it. If the strings of the violin be injured, or if they be smeared with grease, the result is discords and crazy sounds. If the brain be physically injured or disordered the result is what we call mental derangement.

To say, then, that the brain is the *seat* of thought is not at all to say that it is the *source* of thought. Everything involved in my conscious personality is *related to* the brain, but it is not *originated* by the brain. The mysterious spiritual " I " is behind the brain, using the brain —nay further—actually educating and fitting the brain for its work. The brain of a little child with its plastic gray matter is smooth and unformed. It is the "I" behind that is steadily creasing and moulding and training it for its purpose. I don't know of anything more impressive than the study of the human brain in its activities, and how "I" am continually changing and modifying and educating my brain. You feel sometimes as if you could almost lay hands on that mysterious spiritual being that is behind it, like a spider in his web —feeling and interpreting every quiver of it, sending messages out into the world by means of it. But he always eludes you. You have no instrument that can touch him. You only know that he is there, enshrouded in mystery, a supernatural being not only using the brain but educating it for use. The brain itself has no knowledge or thought, and no power of itself to originate knowledge or thought. The brain of a baboon differs very little from the brain of a man. The difference is in the being who is behind it. I read lately the statement of a great scientist: "As far as I can see, if the soul of a man could get behind the brain of an ape he could probably use it almost as well as his own."

I have never known a really thoughtful student of science satisfied with the foolish notion that the brain is what thinks and remembers and wills. He looks upon a human brain, on the dissecting table, a mere mass of cells and nerve centres suffused with blood, and he thinks of the glorious poems and the mighty intellectual efforts and the noble thoughts of God and Righteousness, and perforce he laughs at the thought that that poor bleeding thing originated them. Something within him indignantly replies: "Nay, 'I' am not the brain. I possess it. I use it. It is mine, but it is not me!"

§ 3

We have not yet gone deep enough to discover this "I." It is hardly necessary to ask the next question which some foolish people are speculating about to-day. Am I merely the TRAIN OF THOUGHTS AND FEELINGS AND EMOTIONS? Am "I" but like an Eolian harp, played on by the wind of sensations from without?

Surely not. This mysterious "I" is constantly and persistently claiming to be a real conscious person behind all these—greater than

all these—possessing all these. Listen to the
voice down deep in your consciousness—COGITO,
ERGO SUM. " I " think—therefore " I " exist.
I am not the thoughts and feelings and emotions—I am greater than them all. I am the
possessor of them all. They are mine. They
are not Me. They are only passing phases of
my being. They are always changing. Everything around is changing. I remain the same
being always. Nothing else in the universe remains the same being—except God. God and I.
God and these selves that are in every one of us.

I cannot escape that conviction that " I " am
the permanent being behind all the changes.
No human vision can see me. No surgeon's
knife can detect me. But I am there, behind
everything.

The particles of my body, of brain and nerves
and heart are constantly being changed—every
few years they are completely renewed. I have
had a dozen new bodies, a dozen new sets of
brains and heart since I was born—I am always
wearing them out. I change them when they
are worn out and throw them aside like old
clothes. My thoughts and feelings are ever
changing, like the ripples on the sea.

But I am absolutely certain that " I " am still there—that I am the same—just as God is the same. The same " I " that played as a little child—the same " I " that lived and desired and thought and felt and worked and sinned years and years ago.

Not a particle remains of the brain, or nerves, or tongue, or eyes, or hands, or feet, with which I did a good or evil deed twenty years since— but it is impossible for me to doubt that it was " I " who did it, that I to-day deserve the praise or blame which is due to it.

Every man on earth, when he thinks about it, has this conviction of himself as an " I "—as a person separate from all other persons, as a self separate from all other selves, as remaining always the same being, whatever changes may take place around him. That is what consti- tutes man—a self conscious of itself. As far as we can discover, the lower animals have no such idea. Children, at first, have not. Did you ever notice how a little child never says " I " till he is about three years old? He always speaks in the third person. It is always " Baby does this," " Baby likes that," until the Divine revelation of his personality gradually grows and he recognizes himself as a person. Then, without any teaching on your part, the child, of his own accord, will begin to say " I."

§ 4

Oh, who or what is this awful, mysterious " I " that dwells somewhere in the centre of my being, and rules and possesses and is responsible for everything? What is this self, in each of you, that is hidden behind your faces as behind a mask—that is looking out through your eyes, and receiving, through your ears, the thoughts that others are trying to express for you? Can the surgeon's knife find any trace of it? Is it possible to destroy it? Is it possible to get away from it? It has survived the putting away of every part of the body a dozen times over. Will it survive the final putting away of the whole body at death? Will it survive everything? Shall " I " be " I," the same identical person through all the ages of eternity?

§ 5

Look in again upon this " I " within you and answer this question. Why does it assert so positively that it is impossible to doubt it: " I *ought* to do certain things, I *ought not* to do certain other things"? All over the earth this day—from the St. Lawrence to the Ganges, from the North Pole to the South—there is no man outside of a lunatic asylum without that conviction. No race, not even the lowest, has been found without it. Where did that conviction come from? From the Bible, do you say? From the teachings of Christ? Nay, surely not. Long before the Bible, long before the incarnation of Christ, the old pagan had the thought clear and distinct, though not by any means so clear and distinct as Christianity has made it. Did you ever think of the mystery of this authoritative utterance of the self within you: "*I ought*"? In the very lowest savages it asserts this. St. Paul calls this sense of "ought" —the law of God written in our hearts (Rom. ii. 15). St. John calls it the light of Christ in us, "the light which lighteth every man coming into the world" (St. John i. 9). Longfellow sings of it in "Hiawatha":

> That in even savage bosoms
> There are longings, yearnings, strivings
> For the good they comprehend not;
> That the feeble hands and helpless,

Groping blindly in the darkness,
Touch God's right hand in the darkness.

Even in the heart of the thief or the murderer
it insists : I ought to do this, I ought not to do
that, and when he disobeys this mysterious law
within him he is compelled to drag himself up
for judgment and fierce remorse for wrong that
no one else knows of, that no one else can pun-
ish him for.   What do you think of that mysterious fact about this Conscious Personality
within you ?   Does it not look as if it belongs
to God, that every soul is stamped with God's
image and superscription, as every coin of King
George is stamped in the mint with the image
and superscription of the King ?

§ 6

And this suggests a further question.   Why
is there in us this sense of imperfection, of incompleteness—of ideals always away in the
front that we can never even approximately
reach on earth ?   Look at this conscience which
we have just been thinking about.   It is always
holding high above us an ideal of perfect
goodness and insisting that we must strive
after it.   But we can never get even near it on

earth. The very best man at the close of life
sees his ideal still high above him and feels how
much better he might be and ought to be and
then he dies feeling the incompleteness of this
life. Does not this unfinished life thus broken
off, with its aim still far in the future, demand
something further ? The great German philosopher Kant founded on this fact his famous ar-
gument for Immortality.

Or look at our efforts after knowledge. It
takes nearly all this life to fit the student for
his search after truth, and when he is just ready
and the great ocean of truth lies before him,
Death comes. Oh, how incomplete and unfinished his life seems! Just the scaffolding put
up for his work, just the tools got into good
order. Then he dies.

"For half a century," said Victor Hugo, "I
have been writing my thoughts in prose and
verse, history, philosophy, drama, romance, tra-
dition, satire, ode, song. But I feel that I have
not said a thousandth part of what is in me.
When I go down to the grave I shall have finished my day's work." And this thought of incompleteness compels in him the hope, "another
day will begin next morning."

Was Victor Hugo right ?   Was the old pagan
philosopher right ?   "You may catch my body,"
said Socrates, "but no man can catch me, myself, to bury me."   Victor Hugo did not believe
in the Christian Bible.   Socrates had no revelation from God, except the revelation of this self
within him.   You have the revelation of Christ
as well.   What do you think of the question ?
When the dust shall return to the earth as it
was, shall the spirit return to God who gave it ?
When brain and heart and nerves are destroyed,
when the sun is old and the stars grow cold,
and all that you ever saw is swept away into
nothingness, will this mysterious, lonely self
remain, to say " I " and " my " and " mine "
and " me," through all the ages of Eternity ?

§ 7

Now, I put a closer question still.   Is not this
mysterious " I " behind the brain the being that
God is especially concerned with ?   What He
sometimes calls your soul.[1]   The ceiling of the
Sistine chapel at Rome has a fine paint-
ing by Michael Angelo from the text, " Man

[1] In a simple, popular statement such as this it would but be
confusing to go into nice metaphysical distinctions of soul
and " spirit."

became a living soul." It represents the Supreme Spirit floating in the ether and touching with His finger the body of Adam. As He touches it an electric spark flashes into the body and Adam becomes a living soul. Is not this the centre of the awful mystery that I call "I," myself—the same of which our Lord asks His tremendous question: "What shall it profit a man if he gain the whole world and lose his own self?"

Is not this "self" the real man, the man in the centre of his life, in the deepest recesses of his being, the man as he lives beneath the eye of God and enters into relations with God—the man for whom the Bible announces that exciting adventure in the long ages of the Hereafter?

Is not this "I" looking out from behind your eyes this moment—the real man, of whom the body that you see is only the outward covering, of whom the brain is only the outward telegraphic instrument? Should not we adapt our thoughts to that tremendous fact? Instead of thinking "I *have* a soul," should we not rather think "I *am* a soul"? Instead of thinking, that beautiful girl has an ugly soul, that insignificant looking man has a noble soul, should

we not rather think, that ugly soul has a beautiful girl body, that splendid soul is in a mean
looking body? Would not some such manner
of thinking help to bring home the reality, that
"I" am the invisible immortal being which
clothes itself in a material body during this first
stage of its life. Should not we be more likely
to become acquainted with our own soul, to become impressed with its existence, to think
about its character? Should we not thus learn
more easily that wealth and clothes and outward appearance are not so important, that the
character, the relation to God is the one supreme thing?

Think out for yourself the answer to that and
to all these questions. I am not going to answer any of them. My purpose here is not
to answer questions but to set you asking
them—not to do your thinking for you, but to
set you thinking for yourselves. Is it the spoil-
ing and ruining of that self within you which
Christ balances against the whole world?

§ 8

Now, have I helped, even in a little way, to
introduce you to yourself—that "self" that is

going out into the great adventure of the Hereafter? If I have, I have done a very good
thing for you. With so many the soul is but a
vague abstraction, belonging to the pulpit and
the sick-bed and the life of the hereafter. But
amid the busy daily life, the real work and
pleasure, the real streets and houses, it is hard
to think of it except as something shadowy and
unreal. My effort here is to take it out of the
region of the vague and unreal and bring it into
the region of every-day, practical life.

Try to respond to my thoughts. Try to get
acquainted with your own self—your own soul.
Try to watch its wondrous life. Try to become
impressed with its existence—to think about its
character. Think whether, when the Bible says
anything about your soul, it means this mysterious being that you call " I." Think whether
this " I " is an emanation from God's nature,
and therefore is intended to be in harmony with
Him. Think whether it must live for ever and
ever, and therefore if its character be not of
enormous importance—if its character-making
be not the one supremely importan⋅ thing in
your life.

Then realize that whether you exa.t or de-

grade it, it is with you for ever. YOU CAN
NEVER, NEVER, NEVER GET AWAY FROM YOUR-
SELF. You will be the very same self after
death as before. I read some time since of the
sinking of a ship and how the captain dived
through the cabin door, and keeping the light
above in view, swam up through the hatchway
and escaped out of the wreck. There is a de-
ceitful expectation in human nature that when
we go down in the sea of death and eternity we
shall in some way escape out of ourselves, swim
away from our own personalities, and thus leave
the ship at the bottom of the sea. If the "I"
meant only the body, that would be true. But
this "I" is where character exists, where love
and desire and will exist. This "I" is the
captain himself. The captain cannot swim
away from the captain. Myself cannot swim
away from "myself." "I" must be "I" to all
eternity. I cannot shake off my character, be
it good or bad.

Realize next what you mean to the God who
created you and lovingly planned for you your
magnificent destiny.

Let the soul within you feel its dignity, its
priceless importance in the eyes of its Maker.

Measure the value of it by what God has done for it.

Why was this world slowly built through thousands of ages ? Just as a platform for this " I " to develop character. Why was the Incarnation and Death of the Everlasting Son of God ? Why is the gift and energy of the Holy Spirit ? Why is the perpetual intercession of Christ in Heaven ? Why is the grace and power of the Sacraments in life ? Why are the boundless prospects opened beyond the grave ?

All for the sake of this mysterious permanent supernatural being that we call " I." Measure I say by what God has done for it, the tremendous value He sets on your immortal soul.

CHAPTER II

THE THREE STAGES OF EXISTENCE

§ 1

NOW, grip with both hands the fact that this life, as you know it, is but one single stage in God's plan for you—the Kindergarten stage, the caterpillar stage of your existence. That in five thousand years that spiritual being looking out from behind the mask of your face to-day will be living still, and feeling still, and thinking still. That what you call death, the end of this career, is but birth into a new and more exciting career, stretching away into the far future, age after age, æon after æon, whose prospect should stir the very blood within us.

There is nothing which so touches some of us as a thing with "makings" in it, a thing with untold potentialities in it, a thing which may come in the future to God only knows what. Talk of the caterpillar which is to develop into the butterfly or the acorn which shall one day

be a mighty oak. Why, these miracles are but
child's play compared with the miracles poten-
tially wrapped up in this poor little self. No
wildest fairy tale can suggest the wonder of its
possibilities as it passes out into the new adventure of the life beyond.

§ 2

Thirteen hundred years ago there was an
eager discussion in the court of King Edward
of Northumbria. The old wattled hall was
blazing with torches and a crowd of eager listeners hung intent on the teaching of the Christian missionaries who had just arrived. At last
a grim bearded old earl rose in his place. "Can
this new religion," he asked, "tell us of what
happens after death? The life of man is like a
swallow flying through this lighted hall. It
enters in at one door from the darkness outside,
and flitting through the light and warmth
passes through the farther door into the dark
unknown beyond. Can this new religion solve
for us the mystery? What comes to men in
the dark, dim unknown?"

Perhaps he was thinking of his dead wife or
his brave boy killed in battle. The old earl's

question is the question of humanity in all ages
gazing out into the darkness after its dead.
The full answer can only be had by dying.
But a partial answer can be had now.

The Bible reveals to us that there are three
stages of human existence:

1st.   *The earthly stage*, where " I," the mysterious " I," live with a body woven around me.
The Bible hints that this stage is of untold importance.   In fact, all the future stages depend
largely on how it is lived.   That is what makes
this first stage so awfully important.   It is the
formative time whose influence spreads out into
eternity.   In this stage Acts make habits.
Habits make character.   Character makes Destiny.

2nd.   *The intermediate life* BEFORE THE JUDG-
MENT, THE " NEAR HEREAFTER " WHEN " I "
LAY ASIDE THE BODY AT DEATH.   THIS IS THE
STAGE BEFORE THE RESURRECTION WHICH IN
OUR LORD'S TIME THE JEWS CALLED HADES,
AND IN WHICH THEY CALLED THE SPECIAL
STATE OF THE BLEST PARADISE, ABRAM'S BOSOM,
UNDER THE THRONE, ETC.

3rd.   And away after this the *final stage* the
" Far Hereafter " in the " end of the age," as

our Lord says, where come the General Resurrection, the Judgment of Men, the final stages
of Heaven and Hell. *That stage has not yet
arrived in the history of humanity.*

§ 3

In Part I of this book we are only concerned
with the Intermediate Life, the life of the near
Hereafter which comes after Death and before
the Judgment. We are to study what can be
known about it.

With educated people it should not be necessary to combat the foolish popular notion that
at death men pass into their final destiny—
Heaven or Hell—and then perhaps thousands
of years afterwards come back to be judged as
to that final destiny! To state such a belief
should be enough to refute it. Those who hold
it "do err not knowing the Scriptures." For
the Scriptures have no such teaching.

The Jews in our Lord's time believed in a
waiting life of departed souls before the Judgment. Owing to vagueness and contradictions
in the Rabbinical teaching it is impossible to
state their notions about it with definiteness.
But in the main it may be said that when they

speak of that life as a whole without distin-
guishing between the states of the good and
the evil they call this whole by the general
name of HADES, *i. e.*, " the Unseen " (the Hebrew
word was Sheol), but they also distinguished in
it the abode or state of the Blest as PARADISE,
or the " Garden of Eden," or " ABRAHAM'S
BOSOM," or " UNDER THE THRONE," *e. g.*,
" Abraham whom God planted in the Garden of
Paradise," " our master Moses departed into
the Garden of Eden." The holy Judah rests
this day in " Abraham's Bosom."

Their teaching is of course not authoritative
for us. Doubtless many of their notions on the
subject needed much correction. But our Lord
gives His sanction in the main to their belief
and uses their very phrases in speaking of
the new life, *e. g.*, Dives " in HADES (not Hell,
see R. V.), lift up his eyes being in torment "—
Lazarus " was carried by the angels into ABRA-
HAM'S BOSOM." " To-day thou shalt be with
Me in PARADISE " is His promise to the dying
thief. And it is clear that He did not mean the
final Heaven for He says, " No man hath ascended into Heaven only the Son of Man who
is in Heaven." Even He Himself did not go to

Heaven when He died, for this is His statement after the Resurrection, "I have not yet ascended unto My Father." Where, then, did His Spirit go? The whole Church throughout the world repeats every Sunday, in the creed, "He was dead and buried, and descended into HADES" —the life of the waiting souls. St. Peter tells us in his first Epistle that in those three days Christ's living Spirit went and preached to the spirits in safe keeping who had been disobedient in the old world. For which cause he says, "was the Gospel preached to them that are dead." The same thought was evidently in his mind in his first sermon (Acts ii. 31). "David," he says, "prophesied of the resurrection of Christ that His soul was not left in Hades."

<h2 style="text-align:center">§ 4</h2>

And this is the point of view of all the New Testament Scriptures. Heaven and Hell are always spoken of as states *after the Judgment* and the Judgment is to be in the "end of the world" or the "end of this age."

The great crisis of expectation set before men is not death, but "the Day when the Lord shall appear," *e. g.*, "That ye may be saved in the

Day of the Lord," "The Day of the Lord is as a thief in the night," "Looking for and hasting to the coming of the Day of God," "Keep the commandment till the appearing of our Lord," "To be found with praise at the appearing of Jesus," etc., etc. Warning, reproof, exhortation, encouragement are all directed to that great day at the end of the Waiting Life —the Judgment at the second coming of the Son of Man.

Naturally this belief passed into the thought of the early church. "The souls of the godly abide in some better place and the souls of the unrighteous in a worse place expecting the time of judgment. . . . These who hold that when men die their souls are at once taken to heaven are not to be accounted Christians or even Jews" (Justin Martyr, A. D. 150, *Dialogue with Trypho*). "The souls of Christ's disciples go to the invisible place determined for them by God and there dwell awaiting the Resurrection" (Irenæus, *Against Heretics*, A. D. 180). "All souls are sequestered in Hades till the Day of the Lord" (Tertullian, *De Anima*, A. D. 200). "Let no man think that souls are judged immediately after death; all are detained in one common place of safe keeping till the time when the Supreme Judge makes His scrutiny" (Lactantius, *Div. Institutes*). " During the interval between death and resurrection men's souls are kept in hidden receptacles according as they severally deserve rest or punishment" (Augustine).

Does it not all give a fuller meaning for us to the words of our Lord, " In My Father's house are many mansions " (or abiding places).

This whole teaching about the Intermediate Life has been obscured in our day by the fact that most people read the Authorized Version of the Bible where the word Hades has been unfortunately translated " Hell," just the same as the darker word Gehenna. At the time of the translation of the Authorized Version the old English word *hell*—the hole—the unseen, had not yet stiffened into the awful meaning that it has attained in our day. It was not then a word set apart to designate the abode of the lost. It simply meant the " unseen place," " the covered place." In the south of England still a thatcher who *covers in* a house is called a " hellier." Even in games it was used. In the old English games of forfeits, on the village green, the " hell " is the hidden place where the girls ran away to escape being kissed. You can see it had no awful meaning necessarily connected with it. Therefore it did not seem repulsive to translate the Greek word " Hades," the Unseen, by the English " Hell." But it has become very misleading in later days, and our own conservative instincts which prevent our altering the word in the creed has helped to perpetuate the error.

The revised version has put all this right, *e. g.*, " His soul was not left in Hades (not hell), nor did His flesh see corruption " (Acts ii. 31). " I have the keys of death and of Hades " (Rev. i. 18). At the end of the world " death and Hades gave up the dead " (Rev. xx. 13). In Hades (not hell) ",the rich man lifts up his eyes, being in torment " (St. Luke xvi. 23).

§ 5

The Bible, then, teaches to every careful student that there is the Intermediate Life beyond the grave, a vivid conscious life. That all men go there when they depart this life. No man has ever yet gone to Heaven. No man it would seem has ever yet gone to Hell. No

man has ever yet been finally judged. No man
has ever yet been finally damned. Thank God
for that at any rate. The Bible teaches that all
who have ever left this earth are waiting yet—
from King Alfred to King Edward ; from St.
Paul to Bishop Westcott ; from the poor struggler of the ancient days in the morning of his
tory to the other poor struggler who died last
night.

We are now to study this next stage of our
history, beginning at what we call death which
is really birth into the next stage of life, just as
the death of the caterpillar is the birth of the
butterfly. In this next stage are living to-day
our dear children and brothers and sisters and
wives and husbands within the veil. In a very
few years we shall all have gone through—each
of us just the same " I."

The Bible does not reveal very much about it
as was to be expected. The Bible is intended
to guide our conduct and prepare us for a final
Heaven. Therefore it busies itself with the
responsibilities of this present life and the glories
of the final prospect—touching very lightly the
intermediate stages, just as we press on a boy
the importance of his school days and the high

prospects for his manhood, touching very little the stages between.[1]   But there is much more to be learned from Scripture about this Intermediate Life than most people think.

[1] There is a further reason as regards St. Paul's epistles, which form one-third of the whole New Testament. The reason is that St. Paul and his people were not greatly interested in the Intermediate Life. They looked for the Lord's coming in glory during their own lifetime. Even if some died before, the intermediate waiting time would be so short that it excited no absorbing interest. They did not dwell on it. It could not concern them as it concerns us.

CHAPTER III

WHAT THE BIBLE SAYS ABOUT THE NEAR HEREAFTER

WE are now to enquire about that life into which our departed ones have gone from us. " I " has gone on his mysterious journey into the strange, new land. We are standing in the darkened death chamber, where the dead body lies, with close shut eyes, like an empty house whence the tenant has gone out, closing the windows after him, and the sobbing friends are feeling the inevitable pressure of the questions, " Where is he ? What is he doing ? What is he seeing ? Can we know anything at all about his condition now ? "

Many of them say, " No, we cannot know anything ; all is vague, shadowy, unreal. It is vain to torment our hearts by thinking." So they lock away his photographs and letters, and they gradually, reluctantly let him drop out of their conversation and their prayers, and, as far as possible, out of their thoughts, trusting sadly

41

in the healing influence of time and forgetful-
ness to quiet the aching questions in their
hearts. Ah! it is a poor comfort!

Some of them even think that there is something presumptuous in intruding into mysteries
which they say God has not revealed. "Do
not the secret things belong unto the Lord our
God?" What a pity they do not complete
that text, "But the things that are revealed
belong to us;" and then go on to find out
whether, after all, God has not revealed a great
deal more than they think about that mysterious journey on which the beloved one has gone.
A reverent curiosity concerning the life of our
departed is surely not displeasing to God. "I
would not have you to be ignorant, brethren,"
says St. Paul, "concerning them that are
asleep."

I wish I could comfort those sorrowing ques-
tioners, as I have comforted myself, by thus
searching for what God has revealed. I do not
want to offer mere sentimental guesses. I want
to find for them the "things that God has revealed," and if I draw some conclusions which
I cannot definitely prove from Scripture, they
are only such as seem to me reasonable and

probable from a fair consideration of the evidence, and I shall draw a clear distinction between the authoritative teaching of Scripture, which you are bound to accept, and any conclusions which I draw from Scripture, which you are free to reject.

Let me first put your questionings into clear, definite shape, as you look upon the face of your dead. Is it a life of sleep and unconsciousness into which he has gone, or is he as fully alive and conscious as he was an hour ago? Is there further probation in that life? Is there growth and progress? Does he still remember? Does he still love? Does he still know or care anything about the old home and about us who are left behind? Can he help us? Can we help him? Are we to think of him as one gone absolutely into the unknown, or may we think of him as we do of our other absent one who went to India last year, only with the difference that one writes home and the other does not?

As in all our troubles, we had best go first to our Lord. As He is the only one who really knows all the questions of our hearts, so He is the only one who really knows the secrets of the invisible world. He is the only one on earth who has ever gone away into that strange land and then came back to tell us anything about it. In all things He is our great fore-runner. He, the Son of Man, has gone before us poor sons of man in all the experiences of life,—childhood, youth, manhood, temptation, struggle, sorrow, disappointment, victory, joy. And He has gone before us, too, into the Un-seen Land, as if to lead us and say to us " Be not afraid."

He does not speak much about it. As I have already shown you, this was to be expected. In the first place, in our present imperfect, limited condition, with senses fitted only for this poor earthly life, it would probably be im-possible to teach us anything definitely about the higher life of the spirit world. How can you teach a blind, deaf man about this world of beautiful sights and sounds in which you are living ? How could God teach us definite de-tails about a life which no experience of ours can help us to imagine ? And, besides that, Scripture is intended to guide our conduct in this world, not to gratify our speculations about another world.   At any rate, there is a marked reticence and reserve all through the Bible in speaking of the Hereafter, which reticence and reserve we shall do well to imitate.

§1

First, watch our Lord draw the curtain a little in His story of the Rich Man and Lazarus. The "story" I say, not the "parable." It is no parable. A parable is the statement of an analogy between visible things and invisible. This is a direct statement about the invisible things themselves. Jesus is telling what happens after death. Indeed, many in the early Church thought, and many to-day think, that this is a direct historical account by Christ of the life of a certain selfish rich man in Jerusalem whom He knew and of a certain beggar that lay at his gate. They died and were buried, and those who followed them to the grave could see no further. But the Lord is watching them still as they pass into the land which He knew so well. Whether this was the story of a certain man, or only a general statement about all such men, does not matter.

Christ was telling of what happens just after
death, when the " I," the self, has laid aside the
body and gone out into the Unseen.

I do not mean that this story is intended as a
revelation of that life. If it were it would
doubtless have been more complete. It is
simply a passing reference to it in warning
against the danger of a selfish life. But it lifts
the curtain a little bit.

§ 2

Be quite clear about this—that our Lord
is not speaking of the FAR Hereafter—of the
final stage of human life at the end of the
world, in which after the Final Judgment
come Heaven and Hell. He is speaking of the
near Hereafter, the life immediately after death.
We have seen that there are three stages in our
history :   1st.   This Earth life, where the " I,"
the self, has a body woven around it.   2nd. The
Intermediate Life before the Judgment, into
which I go at death without my body into my
second stage of being. 3rd. The final stage
at the end of the age in which come the Final
Judgment and Heaven and Hell, which stage is
still in the future for all humanity.

Clearly our Lord is speaking of the Intermediate Life, of the unseen life existing to-day,
running on side by side with the earthly life.
For you see the men He speaks of are not long
dead. Dives' brothers are still living here.
Dives is quite conscious that the ordinary life
of men is still going on on earth side by side
with that other life. Clearly Jesus is telling of
the present stage in the life of the departed—
that life in which all our dear departed ones are
living at this moment.

§ 3

Next I notice that that life in its inmost experiences seems very like this life, and follows
from it quite naturally. He depicts it as a
clear, conscious life. They are not dead nor
asleep nor unconscious. They are very much
alive. He represents them as thinking and
speaking and feeling. Lazarus is feeling " comforted." Dives is feeling "tormented," and
thinking keenly of his own misery and of his
brothers' danger on earth at that moment. So
actively alive are they all to him that he wants
one of them to go back to earth to tell his
brothers about it.

Be quite clear about this. Challenge every statement as I go on. Is this a mere speculation of mine or have we Christ's authority for saying that in the new environment men are living a life as clear and vivid and conscious as on this earth—that death makes no break?

§ 4

Next I learn that each feels himself the same continuous "I" that he was on earth. Lazarus feels himself the same Lazarus, Dives feels himself the same Dives, the brother of those five boys. I shall still keep on saying "I." I am not somebody else over there. That is what Jesus said from the other side of the grave—"Handle Me and see—it is I, Myself."

§ 5

Next I read on His authority that there is no break in memory. Of course there could not be if I am still "I." But our Lord confirms this. Lazarus remembers Dives. Dives remembers Lazarus so well that he wants him to go back to convert his brothers. Aye, he remembers the brothers in the old Jerusalem home, the five boys that grew up beside him.

He remembers sorrowfully that they have grown to be selfish men like himself, perhaps through his fault. He is thinking about them and troubling about them. And Abraham assumes this memory as a matter of course. "My son, remember that thou in thy lifetime, etc."

Does not all this confirm our statement in Chapter I, that memory is something more than impressions on the gray matter of the brain; that memory is in the man himself who is behind the brain and, therefore, must go on with him.

§ 6

I read on, "Now he is comforted and thou art tormented." That again is just what I should expect. It is all quite natural. If "I" am still the same "I" in full vivid conscious life, in full memory of the past—if I have passed out of the mists of earth into the full light of the Eternal, where everything is seen at its full value, where money counts for nothing and love counts for everything, it is of course natural that the good man should feel comforted and the bad man should feel tormented.

Only more so. Only more so. That is the difference. The poor humble follower of Christ, even on earth, is in the main happy—at his best moments. But he is not always very happy. He has the inner comfort of the peace of God. But there is much worry and distraction, about his business and his sickness and his troubles of many kinds to spoil his peace. All these earthly troubles are gone now. He sees Christ. He knows of the boundless joy before him by and by. He is comforted.

And I read that Dives " is tormented." Here again all is natural and as we should expect. The godless man is in some degree tormented in this life—at his best moments, when he stops to think, when he lies awake in the lonely night and conscience speaks to him. But there are many distractions to ease his pain—the pleasures and amusements of life, the company of friends, the pursuit of business, the excitements of ambition. So he can manage a good deal to forget God, to acquire a distaste for God, and yet to dull the still small voice that hurts him. But these distractions are gone now. He has gone out into the new life, naked, alone. All the money and business excitement are gone. All

the things of sense and appetite are gone.
That poor soul of his, dwarfed and degraded,
stands in the dread loneliness before God, full
of the sense of loss and misery—of shame for
the past—of dread of what is to come—of
wretched discord between himself and all that
is good.   In Hades, says Christ, not in Hell (the
Revised Version puts that right), in that life
just after death, he lifted up his eyes, being in
torment.   The Judgment has not come yet.
He is not in Hell. Hell has not yet come.
Those things are in the final stage of being.
But already, just after death, Christ says, he is
in torment of soul.

§ 7

I do not think we should pass over the expression "carried by the angels into Abraham's bosom."   Notice that our Lord makes it
simple and intelligible for the Jews by using
their own phrase, " Abraham's Bosom," their
name for the state of the faithful departed immediately after death.   And He says, Lazarus
" was carried by the angels."   If anybody else
but Jesus had said it, we might pass this over
as a piece of poetic imagery.   But it was Jesus

who said it. He says so much about the angels.
He says that there are guardian angels of the
children. He says that the angels rejoice over
one sinner that repenteth. He would not say
this about Lazarus carried by the angels unless
it meant something real. If so I think we have
here our Lord's authority for the ministry of
angels at death, an indication that the poor soul
does not go out solitary into a great lone land
—that there are loving watchers around the
death-bed "sent forth to minister to the heirs of
salvation."

§ 8

I do not know how much weight we should
attach to the suggestion that Dives seems the
better for the discipline of the new life. His
selfishness on earth bulks largely in the story.
Now in all his trouble he is thinking of his five
brothers "lest they also come to this place of
torment."

§ 9

The next words suggest a very serious and
awful question. Is the destiny and the condition of every soul fixed forever at death?

What is the meaning of the phrase : " Between us and you there is a great gulf fixed " ? That is too large a question to deal with here. I postpone it to a later chapter. I have already reminded you of the tremendous importance of this life in its bearing on our final destiny.

III

We get another hint of the Unseen Life in the story of the Transfiguration, when Moses and Elijah, two of the greatest souls of the old world days in the wondrous Waiting Life, come out from that life to meet the Lord and to speak with Him " of His decease, which He should accomplish at Jerusalem " (Luke ix. 31). Does it not suggest at once the deep interest which they and their comrades, the great souls within the Veil, were taking in the mighty scheme of Redemption that was being worked out on earth ?   Does it not suggest that in the spirit land they are watching our doings here ? Does it not help us to anticipate the joy in that wondrous life when, straight from the Cross, Christ the triumphant victor " descended into Hades " (Apostles' Creed) to proclaim the glad news to the dead (1 Peter iv. 18); to unfurl His banner and set up His Cross in the great world of the departed ?

IV

Our next hint comes when the Lord is dying on the Cross. The penitent thief is hanging beside Him. Death is drawing near. The poor sinner is about to take the leap off into the dark. He does not know what is before him: Darkness — unconsciousness — nothingness — what? He does not know. The only one on earth who does know is on a cross beside him. "Lord, REMEMBER ME WHEN THOU COMEST IN THY KINGDOM." And Jesus said: "TO-DAY THOU SHALT BE WITH ME IN PARADISE." Not in Heaven, but in Paradise—the Jews' word for the resting place of good men after death. Now, when one man says to another at such a time, "To-day you shall be with me," surely it suggests, "You and I will be living a full, conscious life, and you will remember our acquaintance here upon the earth; we shall know each other as the two who hung together this morning on calvary." Does it not, at least suggest, recognition in the Unseen Land?

CHAPTER IV

WHAT THE BIBLE AND THE CHURCH SAY ABOUT THE NEAR HEREAFTER

ONLY three hours later the Lord passed through into that Unseen Land. "Father, into Thy hands I commend My spirit, and having said this He gave up the ghost," and departed on the mysterious journey. If we could know anything about what He saw and did on that mysterious journey surely it would give some hints about our dear ones departed.

§ 1

That journey of the Lord into the world of the dead has been made a great article of the Christian faith. We all repeat it regularly in the Apostles' Creed, " He descended into Hell." I need not translate that clause. Every well taught Sunday-school child knows its meaning. " He descended into Hades," into the world of the departed in the great waiting life before the

Judgment. But there is a great deal more than this to be said about it.

Now, let us consider this statement. Clearly it deals with the three days between our Lord's death and resurrection. Where did His spirit go? "To heaven, of course," somebody says. "No," says the Lord Himself after the resurrection, "I have not yet ascended to My Father." Where, then, did His spirit go? "Nobody can tell," you say. Yes, one person could tell, and only one—the Lord Himself. He only could have told of His solitary temptation in the wilderness, and He evidently told it. He only could have told of the solitary scene in Gethsemane, it would seem that He told it. He only could have told of His visit to the world of the dead, and I think that He told it. You remember that after the resurrection He was with them "forty days teaching the things concerning the Kingdom." I think He must have told them then of those three days. Why? Because the knowledge of it was so wide-spread in the early Church, and there was no one else to tell it. Some people seem to think that there are only some obscure verses of St. Peter and a few references of St.

Paul in favour of such teaching. Not at all.
It was the belief of the whole Church. St.
Peter and St. Paul were only two in a crowd
of teachers of early days who proclaimed
triumphantly the visit of the Lord into the
world of the dead. St. Peter seems to be thinking of it in his first sermon when he quotes:
"His soul was not left in Hades" (Acts ii. 31).
Therefore St. Peter knew that it was into that
intermediate life—not into that final Heaven—
that our Lord went at death. This statement
by itself would not prove much, but when I
find the same St. Peter long afterwards telling
so circumstantially in his first epistle (iii. 18)
that when his Master was put to death in the
flesh He was made more alive in the spirit, in
which spirit He went and preached to the spirits
in prison who had been disobedient at the flood.
"For which cause (chap. iv. 6) was the gospel—
the glad news—preached to them that are dead,"
I think it is a fair inference that St. Peter had
some definite information. And then I find
St. Paul, in Eph. iv. 9, when he is writing of
the gifts bestowed on the Church by her ascended Lord. The word "ascended" causes
him to pause abruptly. Men must not think

that His work in the unseen was limited to that work for us in Heaven after His ascension. "Now that He ascended, what is it but that He descended first into the lower parts of the earth (*i. e.*, the world of the departed) that He might fill all things." Hades and Heaven had alike felt the glory of His presence.

And then immediately after the Apostles' days I find the knowledge wide-spread in the Church. I read the writings of the ancient bishops and teachers of the Church, beginning at the death of St. John, the very men to whom we refer for information as to the Baptism and Holy Communion and the authenticity of the four Gospels, and there I find prominently in their preaching the gospel of our Lord's visit to the world of the departed.

§ 2

The earliest is known as Justin Martyr. He was born about the time of St. John's death, and he feels so strongly about the Descent into Hades that he actually charges the Jews with mutilating a prophecy of Jeremiah foretelling it.

Irenæus, the great Bishop of Lyons in France, a little while later tells how the Lord descended into the world of the dead, preaching to the departed, and all who had hopes in Him, and submitted to His dispensations, received remission of sins.

Then away in Egypt comes St. Clement of Alexandria, born about fifty years after St. John's death. I have been greatly interested in some little touches in his chapter on the descent into the world of the dead. He asserts as the direct teaching of Scripture that our Lord preached the Gospel to the dead, but he thinks that the souls of the Apostles must have taken up the same task when they died, and that it was not merely to Jews and saints, but to heathen as well—as was only fair, he says, since they had no chance of knowing. Don't you like that honest appeal of his "as was only fair"?

St. Clement's great disciple, Origen, comes next. His evidence comes in curiously. A famous infidel named Celsus, knowing of this wide-spread creed of the Church about the preaching in Hades, laughs at the Christians. "I suppose your Master when He failed to persuade the living had to try and persuade the dead?" Origen meets the question straight out: "Whether it please Celsus or no, we of the Church assert that the soul of our Lord, stript of its body, held converse with other souls that He might convert those capable of instruction."

Then away in Western Africa, the Church's belief is represented by another great teacher, Tertullian. In Jerusalem, Cyril the Bishop, teaches the people in his catechetical lectures this faith of the Church with a ring of gladness and triumph. He sees Christ not only amid the souls who had once been disobedient, but also in blessed intercourse with the strugglers after right who had never seen His face on earth. He pictures how the holy prophets ran to our Lord, how Moses, and Abraham, and Isaac, and Jacob, and David, and Samuel, and John the Baptist, ran to Him with the cry, "Oh, Death, where is thy sting? Oh, Grave, where is thy victory, for the Conqueror has redeemed us."

I cannot go on to tell of St. Athanasius and the rest. I have said enough to show you that in the early ages of the Church—the pure loving ages—nearest to the Lord and to the Apostles, the Church rejoiced in the glad belief that Christ went and visited the spirits in the Unseen who had never seen His face on earth.[1]

§ 3

This was one of the gladdest notes in the whole Gospel harmony of the early Church for five hundred years, in the purest and most loving days, the days nearest our Lord and His Apostles. It was a note of triumph. It told of the tender, thoughtful love of Christ for the faithful souls who had never seen Him. It told of the universality of His Atonement. It told of victory, far beyond this life. It told that Christ, who came to seek and save men's souls on earth, had continued that work in the world of the dead while His body lay in the grave. That He passed into the unseen world as a saviour and conqueror. That His banner was unfurled there and His cross set up there in the world of the departed. That the souls of all the ancient world who had never known Him, and WHO WERE CAPABLE OF TURNING TO HIM (*i. e.*, who in their earthly probation,

---

[1] See Plumptre, *The Spirits in Prison.*

in spite of all their ignorance and sin, had not irrevocably turned away from God and good), might turn to Him and live. That the spirits of the old-world saints and prophets had welcomed Him with rejoicing. That even men of much lower place had yet found mercy. That even such men as those who had perished in the flood in God's great judgment, BUT HAD NOT HARDENED THEMSELVES AGAINST HIS RIGHT-EOUSNESS AND LOVE, were not shut out from hope. In the " many mansions " was a place even for such as they. To the teachers of the early Church, I repeat, it was one of the most triumphant notes in their gospel—the wideness of Christ's Atonement.

§ 4

That is what we mean, then, by the descent into Hades. Does it not give a vivid reality to that world that we think of so vaguely? Think of it. Was there ever before or since such a scene, such a preaching, such a preacher, such a congregation? Could the wildest flights of imagination go further? Yet it is all sober fact. Try to picture it for yourselves for a moment. The Lord hanging on the cross,

with His heart full of pain for that humanity
that He was redeeming; and yet surely full
of triumph, too, and glad anticipation. He
was going to show Himself to the poor souls
who in the dark old world days had loved God
and Right. He had finished the work that was
given Him to do. He was leaving His Church
with that blessed gospel of salvation to preach
through the centuries to all souls on earth.
But what of the souls who had gone out
of earth from the beginning of the world
without knowing Him? The Church replies,
through her Bible and through her Creed and
through her early teachers, that the Lord was
not forgetting them. He was about to go
forth in a few moments, "quickened in His
spirit," to bring His glad gospel to the waiting
souls. That was the first great missionary
work of the Church. May we not reverently
see His own anticipation of it in His departing
words as He started on His mission, "Father,
into Thy hands do I commend My spirit" (in
the journey on which it is going). May we not
read it in that "au revoir," not "good-bye," to
the thief beside Him, "To-day you shall be with
Me in Paradise"? May we not dwell on the

wonder and joy and gratitude and love which
must have shaken that world within the veil,
as the loving conqueror came in amongst them ?
And may we not reverently follow Him still in
thought when He returned to earth and, as we
conjecture, somewhere in the Forty Days after
the Resurrection, told His disciples of His marvellous experience ?   I am not laying down this
as a statement of Scripture, but I think it is
a fair conjecture, for how else could they have
learned it ?   And if we are right; think how
the knowledge of it would swell the glad con-
fidence of St. Paul.   " For I am persuaded that
neither DEATH, nor LIFE, nor angels, nor
principalities, nor powers, nor height, nor
depth, nor any other creature, is able to
separate us from the love of God which is in
Christ Jesus our Lord."

§ 5

I think we must see that this teaching of
the Apostles and apostolic men of the whole
early Church is true. People sometimes ask,
" Why, then, is it new in our day ? " The answer is easy. At the Reformation time there
were terrible abuses connected with the

Church's doctrine of the Intermediate Life. The practice of purchased Masses, and Pardons, and Indulgences, and all the absurdities connected with the Roman purgatory, so exemplified in Tetzel's cry, " When money clinks at the bottom of my box a soul is released from purgatory." With such provocation one does not wonder—though one may greatly regret— that the indignant reformers, in sweeping away the falsehood, sometimes swept away also the underlying truth. The teaching about the Intermediate Life, and the old practice of the Church in remembering her faithful departed in prayer, were all put in the background as leading to dangerous abuse ; and so the people, getting no real teaching about it, got the sad habit of trying to forget about the state of their dear ones departed. In their ignorance, they could only guess blindly what the Creed here means. So for centuries this has been the " lost article of the Creed." But this teaching of the Creed is none the less true, because it has been neglected in later days. And if it be true, it is well worth our attention, for it confirms what we have already learned from the previous teaching of the Lord, that the life of the departed is * clear, vivid, conscious life, since Christ could teach them and they could learn.

And it suggests that the departed souls of the old world who had no chance of knowing Him have not by death lost all capacity for repenting and receiving Christ.   Those men that St. Peter thinks of had perished in God's great judgment, but it would seem in their terrible fate they had not hardened themselves irrevocably against God.   Those who do that on earth seem to close the door for ever.   That is the sin against the Holy Ghost—the only sin which our Lord says hath never forgiveness either in this world or in the world to come.   These evidently had still their capacity for repentance.   And this gives one stirrings of hope in the perplexities of God's awful judgments.   Don't be afraid to think this.   There is not one word in Scripture to forbid our thinking it.   It merely means that in the terrible fate which they had brought on themselves they had not utterly hardened their hearts—and Christ had not forgotten them in their misery.

§ 6

Estimate fairly the value of this evidence for our Lord's visit to the Unseen Life.   Do not overestimate it. It is not all Scripture. But all that is not Scripture is the wide-spread belief of the primitive Church which was afterwards crystallized into an article of the Creed. Surely it is enough to deepen our sense of the reality of that Unseen Life. It strongly confirms what we have learned already—that that life is a vivid, conscious life into which "I" go my "self," with my full memory of the past. And do not misread it. It is not offering any hope to wicked men who, with full knowledge of Christ, wilfully reject Him. It tells of men who had never known Him, and has hope only of those "who were capable of receiving Him." There is nothing here to make light of the responsibility of this life.

But this message comes to us to comfort the hearts and strengthen the faith of thinking men and women who are puzzled and perplexed and estranged from Christ by the terrible perplexities of life and of God's judgments as they understand or misunderstand them. You have often thought of the difficulty of reconciling the righteous justice of God with His Fatherly love. You have often thought, in wondering doubt, "Why did Christ come so late in the world's

history ?   What of all the old-world souls who
could not have known Him here on earth ?   For
you know that there is no salvation save by
Jesus Christ.   You have read in the Old Testament of whole nations, men, women and little
children, swept away in one dread destruction.
What of them ?   You have wondered about the
vast heathen world passing in thousands every
day into the Unseen, with no knowledge of
Him.   You have sometimes read the Registrar-
General's return of deaths in your city, and
thought of all the little dead children, brought
up in evil homes ; of sullen prisoners hardened
in the jails ; of grown men and women in the
city's slums who, through the hardening influence of circumstances, had little real chance
of ever being touched by that tenderness of
God's love which leads men to love Him in return.   You know they have not died in Christ.
What of them ?"   If you had to stand at some
death-beds at which some of us have to
stand you would feel as we do the insistent
pressure of that question for all in the ancient
or modern world—the vast countless world of the
dead—who had no real chance of knowing Christ
or being touched by His love here on earth.

> Oh, the generations old
> Over whom no church bell tolled
> Christless lifting up blind eyes
> To the silence of the skies.
> > For the innumerable dead
> > Is my soul disquieted!

Trust them with God, says this teaching of the Creed. Christ will do right by them. Christ does not forget them.

> Trust Him, though thy sight be dim,
> Doubt for them is doubt of Him.
>
> * * * * * * *
>
> Still Thy love, O Christ, arisen
> Yearns to reach those souls in prison,
> Through all depths of sin and loss
> Sinks the plummet of Thy Cross.
> Never yet abyss was found
> Deeper than that Cross could sound.

In these two chapters we have touched on the chief statements in the New Testament and in the beliefs of the primitive Church as to the near Hereafter. There are others of less importance to be referred to as we go on. It seemed well to lay down some basis to proceed on.

CHAPTER V

THE CRISIS OF DEATH

IN an earlier chapter I placed you in imagination in the darkened death chamber, looking on the face of your dead and feeling the keen pressure of the inevitable questions: What has happened to him? Where is he? What is he seeing? What is he knowing in that mysterious world into which he has gone?

That death chamber is the best place on earth for solemn thought about the Hereafter. But when you are thinking only of your own dead and your heart is all quivering in pain and longing you are not in the best condition for cool, clear searching after truth. Imagination and sentiment are apt to run away with reason. The tender tortured woman is apt to believe too easily what the heart longs to believe. The stricken man in his deep numb pain is in danger of yielding to hopeless doubt about it all.

So I lifted you away into a clearer atmos-

phere and sent you searching for definite revelations of God about other people's dead thousands
of years ago, where your heart and affections
were not involved, and where cool, clear reason
had a chance to be heard. We tried to study
impartially what Scripture reveals about the
World of the Departed and how the primitive
Church interpreted that revelation. This gives
us a solid basis to proceed on.

§ 1

With that preparation we come back into the
darkened room again looking into the face of
our dead, trying in perplexity of heart to follow him on the great journey. To avoid confusion we assume here that he died a penitent
man in Christ's faith and fear.

Let me try to enter into your thoughts. Let
me begin at the beginning—Death.

Naturally we all shrink from death—the
seeming shock of sundering soul and body—
the launching out against our will into the re-
gions of the Unexplored—the " land of far dis-
tances " as Isaiah calls it. We are afraid of
that unknown death, for our dear ones—like
children afraid of a bogey on the dark stairs.

We can't help being afraid of it. But ought we to be so MUCH afraid of it? Has not our Lord taught us that there is no bogey on that dark stairs, that he who has just now closed his eyes in death is opening them already into a larger life?

"There is no death, what seems so is transition."

Now think of this "unknown death." Has not Christ revealed to you that this terrible thing that you so fear for him who is gone really only means that at the close of this poor limited kindergarten stage of his history Death has come—God's beneficent angel to lead him into the next stage of being. Why should you be afraid? Birth gave him much, Death will give much more. FOR DEATH MEANS BIRTH INTO A FULLER LIFE. What a fright he gives us, this good angel of God! We do not trust his Master much.

Do you say that you do not know what is before your friend—that it is a "leap off into the dark"? Have we not learned from Scripture already that it is much less of "dark" than some of us thought? And may it not be much

less of a " leap off " than we think—only a
closing of the eyes here and an opening of them
there? May not the birth into that life be as
simple as the birth into this? May not our
fright be like that of Don Quixote when blind-
folded he hung by his wrist from the stable
window and they told him that a tremendous
abyss yawned beneath him. He is in terror of
the awful fall. Maritornes cuts the thong with
gladsome laughter and the gallant gentleman
falls—just four inches! May we not believe
that God reserves just as blithesome a surprise
for us when our time comes to discover the
simplicity, the agreeableness, the absence of
any serious change in what we call dying. I
am not ignoring the pain and sickness of the
usual death-bed. But these are not dying? The
act of dying comes after these. These are but
the birth pangs before the new life begins, the
rough, hard bit of road that leads to " the
wicket gate out of the city."

Pliny, from much clinical observations, declares his opinion that death itself is pleasure
rather than pain. Dr. Solander was delighted
at the sensation of dying in the snow. The
late Archbishop of Canterbury remarked as he

died: "It is really nothing much after all."
Dying itself may be pleasure rather than pain.

We have all noticed that expression of com-
posed calm which comes on the faces of the
newly dead. Some say it is only due to mus-
cular relaxation. Perhaps so. But perhaps
not. One likes to think that it may be something more. Who knows that it may not be a
last message of content and acquiescence from
those departing souls who at the moment of
departure know perhaps a little more than ourselves—a message of good cheer and pleasant
promise by no means to be disregarded.[1]

At any rate does not Scripture suggest to us
in the story of Lazarus—of Moses and Elias at
the Transfiguration—of the dying thief—of the
spirits in the Unseen Life whom Christ visited
at His death—that Death comes not as an
executioner to cut off our departed one from
life and love, but rather as God's good angel
bringing him more than life has ever brought,
and leading him by a path as full of miracles of
soft arrangement as was his birth to heights of
ever advancing existence.

[1] I have here freely adapted some thoughts and phrases
from Edwin Arnold's *Death and Afterwards.*

§ 2

God reveals to us too that the closing of the eyes in the darkness of Death is but the opening them to the light of a larger life, to the vision of the new mysterious real world which the glare of this world obscured. It is just what happens every day when the glare of the sunlight, revealing to us every little flower and leaf and insect, shuts out from us the great universe of God which stands forth in the midnight sky. Do you know Blanco White's famous sonnet? He is imagining what Adam must have felt as the first night fell on the earth. All the beautiful world that he had known for but a day was vanishing from him into darkness. Was the end of all things come already? But lo, a stupendous unexpected miracle! Lo, as the darkness deepened a new and more wonderful world was revealed in the sky, a world which the sunlight had kept absolutely concealed:

Hesperus, with the host of heaven came
And lo! Creation widened on man's view
Who could have thought such marvels lay con-
    cealed
Behind thy beams, O Sun? Or who could find

Whilst flower and leaf and insect stood revealed
That to such countless orbs thou madest us blind !
Why do we then shun Death with anxious strife
If Light can thus deceive, wherefore not Life ?

Yes, life shuts out greater things than light
does. God teaches us that Death is birth, that
what the earth life conceals Death will reveal;
that as the babe's eyes opened from the darkness of the womb to sunlight on this earth, so
will the eyes that close in the darkness of death
open on "a light that never was on sea or
land."

§ 3

And may not this act of dying be much less
lonely than we think ? God sent each of us
into this first stage of existence with mother
and home and loved friends about us. No one
comes into this world to loneliness. Should not
that stir some hope at least that the Father
may take similar care for us in our entry on the
second stage at death ? I hate sentimentalizing
about it. But this is not sentimentalizing. I
have already called attention to our Lord's only
account of a good man's entrance into the Un-

seen. "He was carried by the angels," He said, and I have shown you some reason to think that He meant literally what He said— that the angels who are presented in Scripture as so interested in our life here are equally interested in our transition to a larger life—that loving watchers are around a soul as it passes into the Unseen.

I sometimes wonder, too, how much significance should be attached to the fairly frequent phenomenon of dying people seeming in some rapt vision to see or feel as if meeting them the presence of loved ones gone before. Sometimes these phenomena are very striking. I once thought of asking a religious journal to open its columns to testimony from thoughtful, cool-headed clergy and laity of such experiences at death-beds. It might enable us to judge critically if it could be explained away as mere sentimental fancy or if the evidence were strong enough to suggest an underlying reality. It would need to be very keenly criticized. All allowance should be made, especially in the case of women, for the deceitfulness of pious fancies. But there are some cases which, if their number were large enough, would point much deeper, where there could be no case of sentimental fancies. For instance a young student in one of our city hospitals told me a curious experience lately. A little child under two years old had been rescued out of a fire and was dying badly burned. "I took the little chap on a pillow in my arms," he said, "to let him die more easily. Suddenly he stiffened himself and reached out his little hands and his face beamed with the sort of gladness that a child has in reaching to something very pleasant and in a very short time he died." My informant was by no manner of means a sentimental youth, and he was much struck with the incident. I don't know if there is much evidence of this kind. If so it would count for a good deal in forming our judgment. Our Lord speaks of those whom we have made friends on earth receiving us when we die into the everlasting habitations (Luke xvi. 9). Is it too good to believe that He might have meant some pleasant welcoming on the other side— that perhaps that little child in the hospital that night was really reaching out his little hands to some one invisible to the young student? Let us have no weak sentimentalizing, but on the other hand—is anything too good to believe as to what God might do for poor frightened souls at such a dread crisis of being?

CHAPTER VI

"I," "MYSELF" AFTER DEATH

§ 1

BUT we must not delay at Death. Death is a very small thing in comparison with what comes after it—that wonderful, wonderful, wonderful world into which Death ushers us. Turn away from the face of your dead. Turn away from the house of clay which held him an hour ago. The house is empty, the tenant is gone. He is away already, gasping in the unutterable wonder of the new experience.

> O change! stupendous change!
> There lies the soulless clod.
> The light eternal breaks,
> The new immortal wakes,
> Wakes with his God!

Oh! the wonder of it to him at first! Years ago I met with a story in a sermon by Canon Liddon. An old Indian officer was telling of his battles—of the Indian Mutiny, of the most striking events in his professional career; and

as he vividly described the skirmishes, and battles, and sieges, and hair-breadth escapes, his au-
dience hung breathless in sympathy and excitement. At last he paused; and to their expres-
sions of wonderment he quietly replied, "I
expect to see something much more wonderful
than that." As he was over seventy, and retired from the service, his listeners looked up
into his face with surprise. There was a pause;
and then he said, in a solemn undertone, "I
mean in the first five minutes after death."

That story caught on to me instantly. That
has been for years my closest feeling. I feel it
at every death-bed as the soul passes through.
I believe it will be my strongest feeling when
my own death-hour comes—eager, intense, glad
curiosity about the new, strange world opening
before me.

Not long ago in the early morning I stood
by a poor old man as he was going through
into the Unseen. He was, as it were, fumbling
with the veil of that silent land—wishing to get
through; and we were talking together of the
unutterable wonder and mystery that was only
an hour or two ahead. I always talk to dying
people of the wonders of that world just ahead

of them. I left him and returned to see him
in a couple of hours ; but I was too late, he had
just got through—got through into that wonder
and mystery that I had been stupidly guessing
about, and the poor old worn body was flung
dishevelled on the bed, as one might fling an
old coat, to be ready for the journey. He was
gone. Just got through—and I felt, with almost a gasp, that he had solved the riddle of
life ; that I would give anything, risk anything,
for one little glimpse through ; but I could not
get it. I could only guess the stupendous thing
that had come to him. For all the stupendous
changes that have ever happened here are
surely but trifles when compared with that
first few minutes in the marvellous life beyond,
when our friends pass from us within the
veil, and our hearts follow them with eager
questioning—"What are they doing ? What
are they seeing ? What are they knowing
now ?"

§ 2

More and more of late years I keep asking
those questions at death-beds. I seem to myself
constantly as if trying to hold back the curtain

and look through.   But the look through is all blurred and indistinct.

It must always be so while we are here, with our limited faculties, shut up in this little earth body.   I know certain facts about the " I," the " self " in the Unseen Life, but I have no knowledge and no experience that would help me to picture his surroundings.   I cannot form any image, any, even the vaguest, conception of what that life appears like.   That is why my outlook is so blurred and indistinct.

And this brings me to point out WHAT SORT OF KNOWLEDGE WE CAN HAVE AND WHAT SORT OF KNOWLEDGE WE CANNOT HAVE about that life.   It may help you not to expect the impossible.

You desire to know two things about the Unseen World.

1st.   You desire to know the real life of the " I " himself—consciousness, thought, memory, love, happiness, penitence and such like.

2nd.   You desire to know his outward surrounding, so that you can picture to yourself his life in that world.   That is what gives the interesting touch to your knowledge of your friend's life in a foreign land on earth.

Now the first of these is the really important knowledge, and such knowledge you can have and you can understand because it is of the same kind as the knowledge you already have of him on earth.

The second would be an interesting knowledge, but this knowledge you cannot have, because you have no faculties for it and no similar experience to help you to realize it. It is a law of all human knowledge that you cannot know and cannot depict to yourself anything of which you have had no corresponding experience before.

"I," "myself" which goes into the Unseen is the really important matter, not my surroundings. And the essential knowledge, I say, about that self, about his inner real life in the Unseen you can have and you can understand because the inner life there is of the very same kind as the inner life here. If I am told of full consciousness there, of memory there, of love or hatred there, of happiness or pain there, of joy or sorrow there, I can easily understand it. I have had experience of the like here. There is no difficulty.

But the knowledge of the outward environ-

ment there—what we shall be like, how that
world will appear, how we shall live and move
and have our being in a spiritual existence—all
that deeply interesting knowledge which imagination could use to picture that life and
bring it before us—THAT we cannot have. It
is not possible with our limited faculties and
limited experience. We could not be taught it.
We have no faculties to take it in and no experience to aid us in realizing it. A blind man
cannot picture colours to himself, a deaf man
cannot imagine music. It is not that we
are unwilling to teach him, but that his
limited faculties prevent him from taking in
the idea.

Realize your position then with regard to
the spiritual world. Imagine a population of
blind, deaf men inhabiting this earth. One of
them suddenly gets his sight and hearing, and
lo ! in a moment an unutterable glory, a whole
world of beautiful colours and forms and
music has flowed into his life. But he cannot
convey any notion of it to his former com-
panions. He cannot convey to them the slight-
est idea of the lovely sunset or the music of
the birds. We, shut up in these human bodies,

are the blind, deaf men in God's glorious universe. Some of our comrades have moved into the new life beyond, where the eyes of the blind are opened and the ears of the deaf are unstopped. But we have no power of even imagining what their wondrous experience is like.

I suppose that is the reason why we have no description of Paradise or Heaven except in earthly imagery of golden streets and gates of pearl. I suppose that is why St. Paul could not utter what he saw when in some tranced condition he was caught up into Paradise and that life was shown to him—" whether in the body or out of the body," he could not tell (2 Cor. xii. 4). I suppose that was why Lazarus could tell nothing of these marvellous four days in which his disembodied spirit mingled with the spirits of the departed.

" ' Where wert thou, brother, those four days ? '
    There lives no record of reply,
    Which, telling what it is to die,
Had surely added praise to praise."

I suppose it was all unintelligible to mortal ken when the spirit had come back to the body

it had left.   If, in a crowd of blind deaf men,
one got his sight and hearing for a few minutes,
and then relapsed, what could he tell to his
comrades or even fully realize to himself ?

Thus you see the knowledge that you can
have and the knowledge you cannot have of
that spirit life.   Be content.   God has given
you a great deal of knowledge of that real life
of the self in the hereafter.   If He has so made
you that the other knowledge that would help
you to picture the surroundings is impossible to
you it is best that you should know it.   Be content.   Don't cry for the moon.   Follow your
departed in thought into that life and realize
what you have learned from Scripture about
him.

II

What have you learned ?

First that IT IS A VIVID CONSCIOUS life into
which he has gone.

There are several passages in Scripture which
speak of Death as sleep and which taken alone
might suggest a long unconsciousness, a sort of
Rip Van Winkle life, sleeping for thousands of
years and waking up in a moment at the Judg-

ment Day, feeling as if there had been no interval between.   But a little thought will show
it is a mere figure of speech taken from the
sleeping appearance of the body. "The sleep
of Death " is a very natural expression to use
as one looks on the calm, peaceful face after
life's fitful fever and the long pain and sickness of the death-bed. But no one can study
the Bible references to the life beyond without
seeing that it cannot be a life of sleep or unconsciousness. " Shall we sleep between Death
and the Judgment ? " asks Tertullian. " Why
souls do not sleep even when men are alive.
It is the province of bodies to sleep." This
sleep theory has always been condemned whenever the Church has pronounced on it. Even
the Reformers declare it at variance with Holy
Scripture in spite of the strong feeling in its
favour in their day.[1]

The reader who has followed thus far will
need no proof as to the teaching of Scripture
that the Waiting Life before the Judgment into

[1] Our "39 Articles " were originally 42, and the 40th says,
"They which say that the souls of those who depart hence
do sleep being without all sense, feeling or perceiving till
the Day of Judgment . . . do utterly dissent from the
right belief declared to us in Holy Scripture."

which our dear ones have gone is no unconscious sleep but a real vivid conscious life. So
vivid that our Lord's spirit is said to have been
quickened, made more alive, as He passed in.
So vivid that the men of the old world could
listen to His preaching. So vivid that Moses
and Elias—those eager, impetuous leaders—in
that wondrous life could not be held by its
bonds, but broke through to stand on the
mountain with Christ a thousand years after
their death. So vivid that Lazarus (whom our
Lord describes as in Abraham's bosom) is
depicted as living a full, clear, intelligent life ;
and Dives as thinking anxiously about his five
brothers on earth.

That was surely no unconscious life which
St. Paul saw when he was caught up into
Paradise and heard unspeakable things, nor
was it a blank unconsciousness that he looked
for in his desire " to depart and be with Christ
which is far better " (Phil. i. 23).

Do you want further proof ? Look at our
Lord and the thief on the cross. The two men
had been hanging together dying on the cross,
just about to get through the veil to the world
beyond. The poor thief did not know what

was beyond that veil—darkness, insensibility,
stupor, oblivion. The only one on earth who
did know hung there beside him. And when
the poor dying one turned with the words,
"Lord, remember me when Thou comest in
Thy kingdom," He promptly replied, "To-day
thou shalt be with Me." If any one knew,
surely He knew. If it meant anything, it
meant, "There shall be no oblivion, no unconscious sleeping. To-night, when our dead
bodies lie here upon the cross, you and I shall
live and know each other as the two men who
hung dying together on Calvary." Ah! the
wonder to him as he went in beyond the veil,
as though the Lord would lead him, lest he
should be afraid.

Beyond all question God has revealed to you
plainly enough that your beloved has gone into
a full, vivid, conscious life. He is more alive
to-day than he ever was on earth.

§ 2

What follows? This. If I am fully conscious what am I conscious of? Surely, first
of all I must be conscious of myself, conscious
of the continuity of my personal identity, con-

scious of the continuity of my personal character. I must feel that I am the same " I," I
am still "myself." Death which removes only
the outer covering leaves the Ego just where it
was. No better. No worse. The Bible lays
no emphasis at all on death as making any
change in character. Our Lord assumes the
characters as remaining the same. The mere
act of dying does not alter character. I am
the same I. I have entered into a new environment more favourable for the exercise of
my faculties, more adaptable to the acquisition
of knowledge, more helpful, I trust, to growth
in good. But I am the same " I." As I leave
off here I begin there. I take into that world
just myself as I have made it. If I have made
the best of myself what more should I desire
to take ? Consciousness, Memory, Thought,
Love, Character. If I have not made the best
of myself, if I have acquired a distaste for God,
for holiness, still I take in myself just as I
stand. Think how tremendously solemn that
makes the life here. It is the place of character making for the life there. I can never,
never, never get away from myself. I shall
always be myself. You remember what our

Lord said from the other side of the grave.
"Handle Me and see it is I MYSELF."

It is I myself, the very same self. It is they
themselves, the very same selves whom I loved
and who loved me so dearly. In that solemn
hour after death, believe it, your boy, your
wife, your husband, who is experiencing the
startling revelations of the new life is feeling
that life as an unbroken continuance of the life
begun on earth. Only the environment is
changed. He feels himself the same boy or
man that he was an hour ago, with the same
character, aspirations, desires, the same love
and courage and hope. But oh, what a different view of all things! How clearly he recognizes God's love and holiness. How clearly he
sees himself—his whole past life. If ever he
cared for Christ and His will, how longingly,
wonderingly, he is reaching out to Him. If
ever he loved you tenderly on earth, how
deeply and tenderly he is loving you to-day. In
all the whirl of awe and wonder and curiosity
and hope, love must stand supreme. For "love
never faileth." "And now," says St. Paul,
"abideth Faith, Hope and Love (these three that
abide for ever), but the greatest of these is love."

§ 3

What else have you learned? That HE RE-MEMBERS CLEARLY the old life and the old home and the old comrades and the old scenes on earth. There is no conjecturing about that. That goes without saying if "I" am the same "I" in that world. Personal identity of course postulates memory which binds into one the old life and the new. And the Bible takes that for granted. We saw that Lazarus remembered Dives and Dives remembered Lazarus and remembered his old home and the five young brothers who grew up with him. He remembers that they have grown to be selfish men like himself and is troubled for them. And Abraham assumes it as a matter of course. "My son, remember that thou in thy lifetime," etc. Our Lord comes back from Death remembering all the past as if Death made no chasm at all in His memory. "Go and meet Me in Galilee," He says; "Lo I have told you" (before I died). And the redeemed in the future life are represented as remembering and praising God who had redeemed them from their sins on earth.

So you may be quite sure that your dear

one is remembering you and storing up in his memory all your love in the past. Did your wife ever tell you on earth how happy you had made her? Did the old father and mother now in the Unseen ever thank God for the comfort you had been to them during their declining years? Be sure that in that land of love these will be amongst the most precious pictures in their storehouse of memory.

§ 4

And he has taken with him all the treasures of mind and soul which by God's grace he has won for himself on earth. A man can take nothing of the external things—of gold or lands. Nothing of what he HAS but all of what he IS—all that he has gained IN HIMSELF. The treasures of memory, of disciplined powers, of enlarged capacities, of a pure and loving heart. All the enrichment of the mind by study, all the love of man, all the love of God, all the ennobling of character which has come through the struggle after right and duty. These are the true treasures which go on with us into that land where neither rust nor moth doth corrupt.

§ 5

And he is " WITH CHRIST."

The Bible teaches that the faithful who have died in Christ are happy and blest in Paradise even though the Final Heaven and the Beatific Vision is still but a thing to be longed for far off in the future. Lazarus is "comforted" after his hard life on earth. " The souls of the righteous are in the hands of God, there shall no torment touch them." " Blessed are the dead which die in the Lord . . . they rest from their labours." But best of all it assures us that they are WITH CHRIST. " Lord Jesus receive my spirit " the dying Stephen prayed as he passed into the Unseen. They are " absent from the body at home with the Lord." They "depart to be with Christ which is far better."

" With Christ." One has to write carefully here. The full vision of the Divine Glory and Goodness and Love is reserved for the final stage of existence in Heaven where nothing that defileth shall enter in, whereas this Intermediate Life is one with many imperfections and faults, quite unready for that vision of glory. But for all that St. Paul believed that

the presence of Christ was vouchsafed in that
waiting land, in some such way we may suppose as on earth long ago.   Only an imperfect
revelation of the Son of God.   And yet—and
yet—oh, how one longs for it !   Think of being
near Him, even in some such relation as were
the disciples long ago.

" I think when I read that sweet story of old,
    When Jesus was here amongst men,
  How He called little children as lambs to His
      fold,
    How I long to have been with Him then."

Yes, St. Paul seems to say you shall be with
Him, you shall have that longing gratified in
some measure even before you go to Heaven.
So that Paradise, poor and imperfect as it is
compared with the Heaven beyond, is surely a
state to be greatly desired.   Some pages back
I wrote with a certain shrinking " No man has
ever yet gone to Heaven."   It is quite true,
and yet I could feel some poor mourner shrinking back from it as he thought of that beloved
one gone.   Nay, shrink not.   Paradise means
the " Park " of God, the " Garden " of God, the
place of rest and peace and refreshing shade.

The Park is not the Palace but it is the pre-cincts of the Palace. Paradise is not Heaven, but it is the Courtyard of Heaven. And (the dearest, tenderest assurance of all) they are with Christ. Is not that sufficient answer to many questions? At any rate the Bible definitely teaches that.

CHAPTER VII

RECOGNITION

§ 1

SHALL WE KNOW ONE ANOTHER IN THAT LIFE? Why not? As George Macdonald somewhere pertinently asks, "Shall we be greater fools in Paradise than we are here?"

This is a perfectly apt retort, and not at all flippant as it may seem at first. It is based on the belief suggested by common sense and confirmed by Scripture that our life there will be the natural continuous development of our life here and not some utterly unconnected existence. If consciousness, personal identity, character, love, memory, fellowship, intercourse go on in that life why should there be a question raised about recognition? True, there are morbid times with most of us when we are inclined to doubt all desirable things, and there are some gloomy Christians who are always suspicious of anything especially bright and hopeful in the Gospel of Christ. But to the normal Christian

man who knows what is revealed and who believes in the love of God, there should never be
any serious doubt about recognition in that
life.

§ 2

Before saying anything about Scripture evidence let me point out that there are some things
that are always assumed by legitimate inference
even without any definite proofs. If I knew
that the inhabitants of Mars were alive, and in
full consciousness, and with souls like mine, and
capable of intercourse with each other—whether
they have bodies or not, I should assume that
they knew one another. I should not wait for
that fact to be definitely stated by a visitor to
Mars who should return to earth. I should assume it without his stating it. Nay, I should
require very strong evidence to make me believe the contrary. Now, the Bible says that
our dear ones in Paradise are alive,—that their
life is a full conscious life, with full consciousness of personal identity, that they remember
the things of the old earth life, that they love
one another, that they can have intercourse together as in the story of Dives and Lazarus.
So far as we can judge, the inner life of the

"I" THERE seems a very natural continuation of his life HERE.

If then, "I" am the same "I," the same person, still alive, still conscious, still thinking, still remembering, still loving, still longing for my dear ones, still capable of intercourse with others, why may I not without definite proof assume the fact of recognition? Surely it should require strong evidence to make me believe the contrary. It is one thing to avoid reckless assertions without any foundation—it is quite another thing to have so little trust in God that we are afraid to make a fair inference such as we would unhesitatingly make in like conditions here—just because it seems to us "too good to be true." Nothing is too good to be true where God is concerned. I do believe that one reason why we have not definite answers to such questions as this is because such answers ought not to be necessary for people who trusted fully in the tenderness of the love of God.

§ 3

Why, even if the Bible were to give you no hint of it, do you not see that the deepest, noblest instincts that God has implanted in us cry out for recognition of our departed; and where God is concerned it is not too much to say that the deepest, noblest instincts are, in a sense, prophecies. This passionate affection, the noblest thing that God has implanted in us, makes it impossible to believe that we should be but solitary isolated spirits amongst a crowd of others whom we did not know, that we should live in the society of happy souls hereafter and never know that the spirit next us was that of a mother or husband or friend or child. We know that the Paradise and earth lives come from the same God who is the same always. Into this life He never sends us alone. There is the mother love waiting and the family affection around us, and as we grow older love and friendship and association with others is one of the great needs and pleasures of life and one of the chief means of training the higher side of us. Unless His method changes we may surely hope that He will do something similar hereafter, for love is the plant that must overtop all others in the whole Kingdom of God.

Again, love and friendship must be LOVE AND FRIENDSHIP for SOME ONE. If we don't know any one, then we cannot love, and human love must die without an object. But the Bible makes it a main essential of the religious life that "He that loveth God love his brother also."

If we shall not know one another, why then this undying memory of departed ones, this aching void that is never filled on earth? Alas for us! For we are worse off than the lower animals. The calf is taken from the cow, the kittens are taken from their mother and in a few days they are forgotten. But the poor human mother never forgets. When her head is bowed with age, when she has forgotten nearly all else on earth you can bring the tears into her eyes by speaking of the child that died in her arms forty years ago. Will God disappoint that tender love, that one supreme thing which is "the most like God within the soul"?

§ 4

There can be no real reason, I repeat, for doubting the fact of recognition unless the Bible should distinctly state the contrary. And so far from doing this the Bible, in its very few references to the Hereafter life, always assumes the fact and never in any way contradicts it.

Notice first the curiously persistent formula
in which Old Testament chroniclers speak of
death. "He died in a good old age and WAS
GATHERED UNTO HIS PEOPLE and they buried
him." "Gathered unto his people" can hardly
mean burial with his people, for the burial is
mentioned after it. It comes between the dying
and the burial. And I note that even at Moses'
burial on the lone mountain top this phrase is
solemnly used. "The Lord said unto him get
thee up into the mount and die in the mount
AND BE GATHERED TO THY PEOPLE." Miriam
was buried in the distant desert, Aaron's body
lay on the slopes of Mount Hor, and the wise
little mother who made the ark of bulrushes
long ago had found a grave, I suppose, in the
brick-fields of Egypt. Did it mean that he
came back to them all in the life unseen when
he was "gathered to his people"?

David seemed to think that he would know
his dead child. "I shall go to him but he shall
not return to me."

Our Lord assumes that Dives and Lazarus
knew each other. And in another passage He
uses a very homely illustration of a friendly
gathering when He speaks of those who shall

"sit down with Abraham and Isaac and Jacob in the Kingdom." And again in His advice about the right use of riches. " Make to yourselves friends by the means of the mammon of unrighteousness that when ye die they may receive you into the everlasting habitations" (Luke xvi. 9). Surely, that at least suggests recognition and a pleasant welcoming on the other side.

I remember well, how in the pain of a great bereavement, His words to the penitent thief came into my life like a message from the Beyond. " To-day thou shalt be with Me in Paradise." I put myself in the place of that poor friendless man taking his lonely leap off into the dark and felt what a joy and comfort it must have been. " To-day we shall be together again at the other side." Not, "I will remember thee," but, "Thou shalt be with Me." Not, by and by when I come in My Kingdom, but " To-day." If anybody knew, surely Jesus knew. If His words meant anything surely they meant we shall be conscious of each other, we shall know each other as the two friendless ones who hung on the cross together.

Then I see St. Paul (though he is referring to the later stage of existence) comforting bereaved mourners with the thought of meeting those whom Christ shall bring with Him. Where would be the comfort of it if they should not know them? He expects to meet his converts and present them to Christ. How could he say this if he thought He would not know them?

I wonder if anybody really doubts it after all. Just think of it! With Christ in Paradise and not knowing or loving any comrade soul! Is that possible in the land of love? With our dear ones in Paradise and never a thrill of recognition as we touch in spiritual intercourse the mother, or wife, or husband, or child for whose presence we are longing! Cannot you imagine our wondering joy when our questionings are set at rest? Cannot you imagine the Lord in His tender reproach, "Oh, thou of little faith, wherefore didst thou doubt?"

§ 5

Sometimes one vaguely wonders, How can there be spiritual recognition? How shall we recognize each other without this accustomed bodily shape? And in the effort to realize the fact of recognition men have made many guesses. But really we know nothing about the "How." We know that the self in that life can think and remember and love. We know that we can still communicate thoughts to each other. Can we not leave with God the "how" of recognition?

In several places Scripture seems to suggest that the souls of the departed are clothed in some kind of visible spirit shape. They are spoken of as not only recognized but in some way *seen* as in the case of Samuel and of Dives and Lazarus and of Moses and Elias at the Transfiguration and of our Lord Himself in the spiritual body after the Resurrection. They seem to be visible when they please and as they please.

But when a mother asks, how then should she know her child who died twenty years ago, one feels that recognition must be something spiritual and not depending on visible shape. Even here on earth much of our recognition is spiritual. Soul recognizes soul. We recognize in some degree good and evil character of souls even through the coarse covering of the body. We instinctively, as we say, trust or distrust people on first appearance. Or again, a slight young stripling goes away to India and returns in twenty years a big, bearded, broad-shouldered man, with practically no outward resemblance to the boy that went away. But even though he strive to conceal his identity he cannot hide it long from his mother. She looks into his eyes and her soul leaps out to him. Call it instinct, insight, intuition, sympathy, what you please, it is the spiritual vision, soul recognizing soul. If that spiritual vision apart from bodily shape plays so great a part in recognition here, may it not be all-sufficient there? In that life where there is consciousness, character, memory, love, longing for our dear ones, and power of communication, is it conceivable that we should have intercourse with our loved and longed for, without any thrill of recognition? Surely not. Instinctively we shall know.

It was not mother that I knew thy face,
It was my heart that cried out Mother![1]

[1] Momerie. Immortality.

§ 6

P.S.—I let these words stand as they appear in the earlier editions of this book. For they are true. But to my mind now there is a far more probable answer. It is this: That it is not you who will have to do the recognizing; at any rate that you will not be first with it.

If it be true, as we have reason to believe (see next chapter), that your dear one there is watching your life on earth, of course he would know you at once. While, year by year, you have been changing from youth to old age he has been near you all the time. He knows you as familiarly as if he had been on earth beside you. Probably he has been waiting and watching as you came through.

And whatever change has passed on him in his new life, surely he too will be easier to recognize when he has claimed you first.

§ 7

Whether this suggestion appeals or no, at any rate we need have no doubt that we shall know one another there. Nay, shall we not know each other there far more thoroughly than we do here? "Now," says St. Paul, "we see in a mirror, darkly, but then face to face. Now I know in part, then shall I know even as also I have been known." St. Paul's thought is of our fuller knowledge of things hereafter. Does it not include also our fuller knowledge of one another? I met this passage lately in a letter of Phillips Brooks: "I wonder what sort of knowledge we shall have of our friends in the Hereafter and what we shall do to keep up our intimacy with one another. There will be one good thing about it. I suppose we shall see through one another to begin with and start off on quite a new basis of mutual understanding. I should think it would be awful at first, but afterwards it must be nice to feel that your friends knew the worst of you and you need not be continually in fear that they will find out what you really are."

I think a simple natural thought such as that seems to bring the idea of spiritual recognition more within our ken. But we must remember that our conjectures about the MODE of recognition have very little basis. The FACT of recognition we may practically assume. The "how" we must leave with God.

"Soul of my soul I shall meet thee again.
With God be the rest."

CHAPTER VIII

THE COMMUNION OF SAINTS

WE have already seen that the evidence of Scriptures leads us to the assurance that our dear ones departed are living a vivid, conscious life ; that there is continuance of personal identity. " I " am still " I," and that there is memory still, clear and distinct, of the old friends and the old scenes on earth.

§ 1

We pass on to consider the relations between ourselves and them. Do they know now of our life on earth ? Can there be between us comradeship in any sense ? Can there be love and care and sympathy and prayer between us on these two sides of the grave, as there is between friends on earth on the two sides of the Atlantic ?

The Church says yes, and calls it in her creed, the Communion of Saints. The Communion of Saints—a very grand name, but it means only a very simple thing—just loving sympathy between us and these elder brothers and sisters beyond the grave.

The term "saint" in the New Testament only means any poor humble servant of Christ "set apart" to Him, baptized into His name. Communion means Fellowship, Comradeship. Therefore the Communion of Saints simply means fellowship between Christians, and in church language has come chiefly to mean fellowship between Christians at this side and at the other side of death. Knowledge and comradeship and sympathy and love and prayer between the church MILITANT on earth and the church EXPECTANT in Paradise, as they both look forward to the final joy of the church TRIUMPHANT in Heaven, and meantime cooperate one with the other to bring the whole world within the Kingdom of Christ.

§ 2

You see that it is a prominent doctrine of the Church's creed, and rightly understood, it is a very beautiful and touching doctrine—not only because of the union of fellowship with our departed—but especially because the bond of that union and fellowship is our dear Lord Himself, whom we and they alike love and thank and praise and pray to and worship, and from whom we and they alike derive the Divine sustenance of our souls.

You know what a bond of union it is between two men even to find that they both deeply honour and admire and love the same friend and benefactor. They become one in him. The Bible means that, but a great deal more, when it says we are "one in Christ Jesus."

Here on earth, there in Paradise, is His presence. Here on earth, there in Paradise, is the love and prayer and praise going forth to Him, and the strength and power of God coming back from Him. You know His own simile, "I am the Vine, ye are the branches." From the central Vine the life rises and flows to every farthest branch and twig and leaf, connecting them all in the one life. He the Sacred Vine is on earth with us and in Paradise with them. Some of the branches are in the shadow here, some of them are in the sunlight there, but we are all united through the Lord Himself. He is the Vine, we are the branches. Because He is with us here, prayer and praise and all the

functions of the Church are here.   Because He
is with them in Paradise prayer and praise and
all the functions of the Church go on in Paradise.   Every Sunday as we in our poor way
love Him and worship Him and pray to Him
and praise Him, our dear ones beyond are doing
the very same.   Notice how in the Communion
Service we remind ourselves of the fact.
" Therefore with angels and archangels and all
the company of Heaven we laud and magnify
Thy holy name," etc.   It is not we alone who
feed on His divine life, it is not the altar on
earth alone that communciates the all-prevail-
ing virtues of the atoning Blood, for the same
Victim is the central object of adoration beyond,
as saints and angels and all redeemed creation are with us taking up together the chorus
of that everlasting hymn.

If we on this side were living closer to our
Lord and closer to our departed, how close
might that comradeship become !   We should
tell our Lord so much about each other.   We
should think of each other and remember each
other and sympathize with each other and pray
for each other.   Why, we could do everything
for each other that we can do on earth when

separated by the Atlantic—except just write
home. (Ah, how one wishes that they could
" write home " !) We are very close if we
would but realize it.

> " Death hides but it does not divide
> Thou art but on Christ's other side,
> Thou art with Christ and Christ with me
> In Him I still am close to thee."

II

Yes, you say, that is a beautiful thought.
But is that all? My poor heart is craving for
more communion than that. Do they know or
care about my love and sorrow to-day? And
are they helping me? Are they praying for
me to that dear Lord whom we both love—in
whose presence we both stand to-day? And
can I do anything for them on my side in this
" Communion of Saints " ?

§ 1

Do they pray for us or help us in any way?
Does any one need to ask that question?

Since they are with Christ of course they
pray. The world to come is the very atmos·
phere of prayer. St. John in his vision tells of
" the offering of the golden vials full of odours

which are the prayers of the saints " (Rev.
v. 8). And again three chapters later the
angel stood to offer the prayers of all saints upon
the golden altar.

Can you imagine your mother who never
went to bed here without earnest prayer for her
boy going into that life with full consciousness
and full memory of the dear old home on earth,
and never a prayer for her boy rising to the
altar of God ?

Why, even the selfish Dives, after death,
could not help praying for his brothers.

Aye, she is praying for you.   I think amongst
the most precious prayers before the golden
altar are the mother's prayers for her boy who
is left behind on earth.

§ 2

But, you say, she does not know anything
about my life or my needs on earth.   Even if
she did not know she would surely pray for you.
But I am not so sure that she does not know.
There are several hints in Scripture to suggest
that she does know—hints so strong that if
you are doing anything now that she would like
I should advise you to keep on doing it and if

you are doing anything now that you would not wish her to know, I should advise you to stop doing it.

Our Lord represents Abraham as knowing all about Moses and the prophets who came one thousand years after his time (St. Luke xvi. 29).

Our Lord distinctly tells the Jews that Abraham in that life knew all about His mission on earth. "Your Father Abraham rejoiced to see My day and he saw it and was glad" (St. John viii. 56).

At the Transfiguration, too, Moses and Elias came out from that waiting life to speak with Christ of His decease which He should accomplish at Jerusalem. Does it not suggest at once that they and their great comrades within the veil were watching eagerly and knowing all about the life of Christ and the great crisis of man's redemption towards which they had been working on earth long years ago. Can any one believe that the whole Waiting Church within the veil, living, and conscious, and thinking, and remembering were absolutely ignorant and unconcerned about the greatest event that ever came in the history of their race?

The writer in the Epistle to the Hebrews apparently believed that our departed ones were watching our course, for after a long list of the great departed heroes of faith in olden time he writes to encourage us in the race on earth. " Seeing that we are encompassed about with so great a cloud of witnesses let us lay aside every weight and run with patience the race that is set before us " (Heb. xii. 1). The picture suggested is that of the runners in the amphitheatre on earth and the galleries of Creation crowded with sympathetic watchers 'ike the " old boys " of a great English school coming back at the annual school games to cheer on the lads and remember how they had run themselves long ago in the very same fields.'

III

And the hope which Scripture thus suggests and never contradicts commends itself to

---

¹ It is true that the Greek word translated "witnesses" is not the word meaning "spectators" but rather "witnesses for the faith," but as most good commentators (including Bishop Westcott) say—it is impossible to exclude the thought of spectators in an amphitheatre watching a race. The Revised Version, too, seems to accept this view for it prints the word "witnesses" without any marginal remark.

reason and to the deepest instincts in our hearts.

I think of a mother leaving her children and going into a full conscious life, where, mark you, she can still think and remember and love. I see that her love for them was probably the most powerful influence in ennobling her life here. And she has gone into a life where that ennobling is God's chief aim for her. Since she can remember them, I feel quite sure that if she had the choice she would want to watch over them always.

But, somebody says, she might not be quite happy if she knew all that they had to go through. Seeing that at any rate she remembers them, do you think she would be more happy if she knew that they might have to go through troubles of which she could not learn anything? Put yourself in the place of any mother on earth that you know and ask if it would make her any happier to stop all letters about her children whom she felt might be in danger or trouble. Are you quite sure that in that spirit life a peaceful contentment like that of the cow who forgets her calf is the highest thing to be desired? The higher any soul grows on earth the less can it escape unselfish sorrow for the sake of others. Must it not be so in that land also? Surely the Highest Himself must have more sorrow than any one else for the sins and troubles of men. Have you ever thought of that "eternal pain" of God? If there be joy in His presence over one sinner that repenteth must there not be pain in His presence over one that repenteth not?

There are surely higher things in God's plans for His saints than mere selfish happiness and content. There is the blessedness that comes of sympathy with Him over human sorrow and pain. We but degrade the thought of the blessedness of the redeemed when we desire that they should escape that.

And since in that life she is "with Christ" and able doubtless to win for her children more than she could ever win on earth, and since she knows that Christ is more solicitous for them than she is herself and that she can trust Him utterly to do for them more than she can ask or think, does it not seem far more probable that she should still know and care and love and pray and share in the care and sympathy of Christ for them?

Yes, I think probably she does know about them. I know certainly she prays about them. I myself hope and believe that some of the best helps in my life have been won for me by those on the other side who love me and who are so near to their Lord.

§ 2

And it is a strong confirmation of that belief when I find it the belief of the great bishops and teachers of the early Church in its purest and most loving days, the days nearest to those of Christ and His apostles.

St. Cyprian the martyr bishop of Carthage who was born in the century after St. John's death (A. D. 200) made an agreement with his friend Cornelius that whichever of them died first should in the Unseen Land remember in prayer him·who was left behind. "Let us mutually be mindful of each other. . . . On both sides let us always pray for each other, let us relieve our afflictions and distresses by a reciprocity of love and whichever of us goes hence before the other by the speed of the Divine favour, let our affection continue before the Lord, let not prayer for our brothers and

sisters cease before the mercy of the Father"
(Ep. lvii. ad Cornel.). And in the days of the
plague at Carthage, A. D. 252, he comforts his
fellow citizens reminding them of "the large
number of dear ones, parents, brothers, children,
a goodly and numerous crowd longing for us
and while their own immortality is assured still
longing for our salvation."

Origen, who was a contemporary of Cyprian,
says, "All the souls who have departed this life
still retaining their love for those who are in
the world concern themselves for their salvation
and aid them by their prayers and mediation
with God.   For it is written in the Book of
the Maccabees, 'This is Jeremiah the prophet
who always prays for the people'" (in Cant.
Hom. iii.).   And in another work he says,
"It is my opinion that all those fathers who
have fallen asleep before us fight on our side
and aid us by their prayers" (in Jesu Nave
Hom. xvi. ch. 19).   And again "They (in that
unseen life) understand who are worthy of
Divine approval and are not only well disposed
to these themselves, but coöperate with them
in their endeavours to please God, they seek
His favour on their behalf and with their

prayers and intercessions they join their own."
And again, "These (in the Unseen Life) pray
for us and bring help to our perishable race,
and if I may so speak, take up arms alongside
of it " (Contra Celsum viii. 64).

St. Gregory Nazianzen is preaching the funeral sermon of St. Basil. " He still prays for
the people," he says, " for he did not so leave
us as to have left us altogether." And in his
funeral sermon over his own father, " I am satisfied that he accomplishes there now by his
prayers more than he ever did by his teaching just
in proportion as he approaches nearer to God
after having shaken off the fetters of his body."

St. Cyril, Bishop of Jerusalem, in his Catechetical lectures, and St. Chrysostom in several
of his homilies speak of the help we get through
the prayers of departed holy men.

St. Ambrose in his great grief at his brother's
death, says: " What other consolation is left
me but this that I hope to come to thee my
brother speedily, that thy departure will not
entail a long separation between us, and that
power may be granted me by thy intercessions
that thou mayest summon me who long to join
thee more speedily."

St. Jerome, who gave us the Vulgate, the great Revised Bible of the Western Church, is comforting a mother who has lost a daughter. "She entreats the Lord for thee and begs for me the pardon of my sins." Again to another friend, Heliodorus, he speaks of the life after death. "There you will be made a fellow burgher with St. Paul. There also you will seek for your parents the rights of the same citizenship. There too you will pray for me who spurred you on to victory." Again he vigorously disputes with Vigilantius who asserts that prayers and intercessions must cease after death. "If the apostles and martyrs while still in the body are able to pray for others . . . how much more may they do so now. . . . One man, Moses, obtains from God pardon for 600,000 men in arms; and Stephen, the imitator of his Lord, begs forgiveness for his persecutors; shall their power be less after they have begun to be with Christ?"[1]

§ 3

But sympathy and prayer must not be on one side only. It must be mutual in the Communion of Saints. They remembering and loving,

[1] Luckock, *After Death.*

and thinking about us. We remembering and loving, and thinking about them. They asking from their Lord blessing for us. We asking from Him blessing for them. For surely they are not above wanting His blessings still—not even the best of them though safe with Him, though forgiven their sins, they are still imperfect, still needing to grow in grace, in purification, in fitness for the final heaven by and by. And we can help their growth as they can help ours.

Some of the most deeply religious people that I know shrink from the thought of prayer for the departed. There has been reason for it. This beautiful old custom, the custom of the Jews, the custom of the whole Christian Church till the Reformation [1] had grown at that time into great corruption. And one danger of great corruption is that indignant reformers are likely to tear away more than the corruption, "hating even the garment spotted by the flesh." So it was here. Because of the abuse men feared even the use. In their hatred of

---

[1] The evidence for this can be seen in full in any standard work on the subject, *e. g.*, Luckock, *After Death;* or Lee, *Christian Doctrine of Prayer for the Departed.*

the sordid traffic in masses for the dead they looked with suspicion on any prayer for the departed. And at length men began to think that such prayers were even wrong.

Ah, it was a pity! Our departed ones have more quickly passed into oblivion. The great Paradise life has almost faded from our view. We are the more lonely in our desolate bereavement. Perhaps our dear ones beyond are the more lonely, too, if they know about our life and our prayers on earth. A friend said to me lately, " I was a little child when the news came of father's death far away. That night in my prayers I prayed for father as usual. But my aunt stopped me. ' Darling,' she said, ' you must not pray for father now; it is wrong.' And I can remember still how I shrank back feeling as if some one had slammed the door and shut him outside."

I think we should be happier and better, I think the Unseen World would come back more clearly on our horizon if we kept our dear ones in our prayers as we used to do before they died. Do not keep any hidden chambers in your hearts shut out from Christ. Bring your dear departed ones to Him as you

bring all else to Him. He knows what is best
for them. Pray only for that. Pray "Lord
help them to grow closer to Thee. Help them
if it may be to help others and make them
happy in Thy great Kingdom until we meet
again." Pray something like that. Oh, how
can you help doing it if you love them and
believe in prayer?

How can I cease to pray for thee? Somewhere
In God's wide universe thou art to-day.
Can He not reach thee with His tender care?
Can He not hear me when for thee I pray?
Somewhere thou livest and hast need of Him,
Somewhere thy soul sees higher heights to climb,
And somewhere, too, there may be valleys dim
Which thou must pass to reach the heights
    sublime.
Then all the more because thou canst not hear
Poor human words of blessing will I pray.
O, true brave heart, God bless thee wheresoe'er
In God's wide universe thou art to-day!

CHAPTER IX

GROWTH AND PURIFICATION

WHAT is the main purpose of the Intermediate Life? Is there something to be done there which cannot be fully done at any other time?

Let us still try to keep to the firm ground of Scripture, and to avoid confusion let us confine ourselves still to the case of those who have died, in some degree at least, in penitence and faith.

§ 1

We have already seen that Scripture intimates that that life is not one of sleep or unconsciousness. It is a clear conscious life. It is therefore natural to ask what happens in it? What is the use of it? Science and experience teach that growth is the law of all the life which we know anything about. Even if we had no further light of revelation we should find it difficult to believe that imperfect beings dying in the grace of God pass into that life and live in it for years or for ages without any growth or development.

Scripture also teaches that God's aim for us is not merely that we should escape hell or just creep into heaven. Our goal is to grow into the likeness of God, to "rise to the stature of the perfect man, even to the stature of the fullness of Christ." How many of us are ever even in sight of that goal when we die?

But Scripture goes further still. It points us forward to the final stage of being, to the Beatific Vision of God in the far future and tells us with awe that that God "is of purer eyes than to behold iniquity," that " even the heavens are not clean in His sight ; " that into that final abode of bliss " nothing that defileth shall enter in." Which of us, the greatest soul of us all, can look forward to such a prospect without bowing himself in dread like Isaiah of old, " Woe is me for I am undone, for I am a man of unclean lips, that mine eyes should see the King of the Lord of Hosts ! " If there be no growth or purification in the Waiting Life what hope is there ever for any one of us of fitness for the presence of the all holy God ?

Think that the great majority of those who

die, even though penitent and striving after
right, have much of evil clinging to them; that
many after a whole life of ingraining their
characters with evil have brought sorrowfully
to Christ at last their poor defiled souls; that
even the best is not without many faults and
stains. If nothing that defileth shall enter
Heaven, if growth is a law of all life as far as
we know it, are we not practically compelled to
believe that much of the growth and purification
needed to fit us for God's presence shall take
place in the great Waiting Life?

And this belief and hope for all these poor
faulty souls in whom the good work of God has
begun on earth, St. Paul confirms. " Being
confident of this very thing, that He who hath
begun a good work in you will perfect it UNTIL
THE DAY OF JESUS CHRIST "—*i. e.*, right
through the earth life, right through the Intermediate Life, until the last great scene in the
drama of our history opens at the Judgment
Day.

§ 2

How this shall take place God has not
definitely revealed to us. But God has given

us reason and common sense to enable us to draw conclusions from what He has revealed. Since in that life I am the same conscious "I," with the same consciously continuous personality, with the same conscience and memory, I may surely expect that the Holy Spirit "who hath begun a good work in me and will continue it until the day of Jesus Christ"— will continue it in much the same natural way as here, through Conscience and Memory and the Sense of His Presence. Only that these will be all more keen and effective and free from the disturbance of the bodily senses and the distractions of this life on earth.

CONSCIENCE here is the throne of the Holy Ghost, from which He rules and directs my life. Therefore my body is "the temple of the Holy Ghost." But Conscience here is greatly weakened by fears and hopes and ambitions and distractions of various kinds. At times, when I lie awake at night and think about my life, or when I enter into my closet to prepare by special concentration of spirit for my Holy Communion, I get some dim notions of what Conscience might effect in me if it had a free hand. In THAT life of close spiritual concentration, when the outer world is shut off and the soul enters into its own deepest recesses, contemplating itself, contemplating its past and its future, contemplating the deep tender love of Him who is there present as in Palestine long ago, and feeling that in spite of all my shameful ingratitude He is loving me and blessing me and watching tenderly over me—surely I may expect great things of the operation of Conscience in me.

MEMORY in this life is a very wonderful thing. It can call up in a moment, for Conscience to work on, pictures of half a century ago. But in the fast crowding impressions on the senses Memory is overtaxed and has to lay away in its storehouse of subconsciousness whole tracts of the past which never rise up before my conscious thought at all. Psychological science has much to say in late years about this storehouse of subconscious memory and the power that, unknown to me, it is exerting on my life. It is there all the time, "under the threshold." These buried memories are alive, ready to spring up, but asleep—in abeyance.

§ 3

Now think what this means for Conscience and for Memory as the handmaid of Conscience in the great contemplative life after Death. There is no good or evil thing that I have ever done but Conscience has pronounced on. Some of these judgments I remember. Some of them I forget. In the many distractions of life and the desire to escape painful thoughts, there has dropped down under the threshold of my conscious thought a vast store of memories of which I am oblivious, but of which one and another and another springs up at times unexpectedly with a startling reminder of the great hidden store behind. I meet by chance an old friend of my boyhood, and as he talks about the old times, picture after picture springs up into the light, memories which had long gone from me and which would never have sprung up from "under the threshold" but for the chance stimulation of his talk.

We have often heard of drowning people on the verge of death having the forgotten memories of half a lifetime flashed back in a moment. An old friend once told me a curious experience. "I was crossing a railway line hurriedly on a wet day. As I rushed over the rails the Express came in view. I slipped and fell—fortunately into a hollow where men had been working, and swift as a flash the Express swept over me. The experience of that half minute I shall never forget. It seemed that my whole life was blazoned before me in thirty seconds. Things that I had not remembered for forty years past flashed back in a moment as if they had happened yesterday."

That is what Memory can do even in this life under strong excitement, calling up its forgotten stores. Think what its power may be in that life as a handmaid to Conscience. With all its old lumber rooms of forgotten deeds thrown open—with all the forgotten feelings of my life—boyhood, youth, manhood—open for my contemplation. My impatience and God's patience, my sorrows and why God sent them, my mercies, all the kindly providences of God working unknown to me all my days.

And my sins—some sins that I hate to think of, some that I had almost succeeded in forgetting, all standing out clearly before me in the unsparing light of that mysterious life.

I sat alone with my Conscience
  In the place where time had ceased.
We discoursed of my former living
  In the land where the years increased.
And I felt I should have to answer
  The questions it put to me,
And to face those questions and answers
  In that dim eternity.

And the ghosts of forgotten actions
  Came floating before my sight,
And things that I thought were dead things
  Were alive with a terrible might.
And the vision of all my past life
  Was an awful thing to face
Alone, alone with my Conscience,
  In that strange and lonely place.

Aye, my Conscience must do its work some day if I keep it from doing it now. But all this will be in the presence of my Saviour. They are " with Christ."

Every memory will be more keen and poignant and yet more peaceful and touching in the presence of that dear loving Lord who I feel knows all and yet has loved and received and forgiven me in spite of all, and who is watching over me with deep tenderness like the refiner of silver over His furnace as the dross is cleared away and I grow steadily in fitness for the glorious life of unselfish joy and service in Heaven.

But pain! You do not like any thought of pain in connection with that life. Yes surely, more or less, according to one's state, and dying gradually into perfect peace. Growth of holiness does not come to sinful man here or there but through pain, the tender blessed pain of God's purification, the pain of self-reproach, the pain that thou hast sinned,

> "The shame of self and pity for thy Lord
>   That One so sweet should e'er have placed
>   Himself
>   At disadvantage such, as to be used
>   So vilely by a being vile as thee."

But what a sweet and wholesome pain, mingled with the sense of safety and peace and hope—mingled with deep joy and boundless adoring gratitude and love as we see the stain of the old sins steadily being effaced and look forward to the sure bliss of Heaven in the future! Surely by means of such pain and gratitude and adoring love God makes sinful souls fit for Heaven.

CHAPTER X

PROBATION IN THIS LIFE

UP to this we have been ignoring a large proportion of the inhabitants of the Unseen Land. To avoid misunderstanding we have kept in view those only of whom we had hope that they died in the fear and love of God. But there is no evading the thought that between these and the utterly reprobate, there are multitudes of Christian and heathen in that Unseen Life to-day who belong to neither class, mixed characters in all varying degrees of good or evil. Of many of them it could be said that those who knew them best saw much that was good and lovable in them. But it could not be said that they had consciously and definitely chosen for Christ.

They must form the majority of those to-day in the Unseen Land. Therefore one cannot help wondering about them. One day death overtook them. The thought of them comes

forcibly when some morning the newspapers
startle us with the story of a terrible battle
or railway smash or shipwreck or conflagration
in which hundreds have passed out of life in a
moment and the horror of the catastrophe is
deepened by the thought that they have been
called away suddenly unprepared.

What of their position in the Intermediate
Life ? Our Christian charity prompts us to
hope the best for them. But are we justified
in hoping? It is impossible for thoughtful,
sympathetic men to evade that question. It is
cowardly to evade it. At any rate a treatise
on the Intermediate Life can hardly pass over
altogether the thought of the majority of its
inhabitants and it cannot be wrong for us humbly and reverently to think about them.

§ 2

I have already pointed out the solemn responsibility of this earth life in which acts
make habits and habits make character and
character makes destiny. I am about to point
out the grave probability, to say the least of it,
that in a very real sense this life may be the
sole probation time for man. But this does not

shut out the question of the poor bereaved mother by the side of her dead son. " If any soul has not in penitence and faith definitely accepted Jesus Christ in this life is it forever impossible that he may do so in any other life ? "

I answer unhesitatingly, God forbid! Else what of all the dead children down through the ages and all the dead idiots and all the millions of dead heathen and all the poor strugglers in Christian lands who in their dreary, dingy lives had never any fair chance of knowing their Lord in a way that would lead them to love Him, and who have never even thought about accepting or rejecting Him ? " Shall not the Judge of all the earth do right ? " Shall not the loving Father do His best for all ? Our Lord knew " that if the mighty works done in Capernaum had been done in Tyre and Sidon they would have repented." Does He not there suggest that He would take thought for those men of Tyre and Sidon in the Unseen Land ? Does He not know the same of many gone unto that Unseen from heathen lands and Christian lands, who would have loved Him if they knew Him as He really is and who have but begun to know Him truly in the world of the dead—of many who in their ignorance have tried to respond to the dim light of Conscience within and only learned within the veil really to know Him the Lord of the Conscience, "the light which lighteth every man coming into the world" (St. John i. 9).

Here is no question of encouraging careless, godless men with the hope of a new probation. Here is no question of men wilfully rejecting Christ. The merry, thoughtless child—the imbecile—the heathen—had no thought of rejecting Christ. The poor struggler in Christian lands, brought up in evil surroundings, who though he had heard of Christ yet saw no trace of Christ's love in his dreary life—he cannot be said to have rejected Christ. The honest sceptic who in the last generation had been taught as a prominent truth of Christianity that God decrees certain men to eternal Heaven and certain men to eternal Hell not for any good or evil they had done but to show His power and glory, and who has therefore in obedience to conscience frankly rejected Christianity—can he be said to have rejected Christ?

The possibility in this life of putting oneself outside the pale of salvation is quite awful

enough without our making it worse.   It is
not for us to judge who is outside the pale of
salvation nor to limit the love of God by our
little shibboleths.   It is on a man's WILL, not on
his knowledge or ignorance that destiny depends.   God only can judge that.   All the
subtle influences which go to make character
are known to Him alone.   He alone can weigh
the responsibility of the will in any particular
case.   And surely we know Him well enough
humbly to trust His love to the uttermost for
every poor soul whom He has created.

II

But this hope must not ignore the solemn
thought that in a very real sense the probation
of this life seems the determining factor in
human destiny—even for the unthinking—even
for the ignorant—nay even for the heathen who
could never have heard of Christ here.   Rightly
understood all that we have said does not conflict with this.   It may seem strange at first
sight to think of the heathen as having any
real probation here.   Yet, mark it well, it is of
this heathen man who could not consciously
have accepted Christ in this life that St. Paul

implies that his attitude in the Unseen Life towards Him who is the Light of the World is determined by his attitude in this life towards the imperfect light of Conscience that he has. " If the Gentiles who have not the Law do by nature the things contained in the Law, these having not the Law are a law unto themselves, which show the works of the Law written in their hearts, their Conscience bearing witness " (Rom. ii. 14).

We may assume that St. Paul means that the heathen man who in this life followed the dim light of his conscience is the man who will rejoice in the full light when it comes and that the man who has been wilfully shutting out that dim light of conscience here is thereby rendering himself less capable of accepting the fuller light when he meets it hereafter. In other words this life is his probation, he is forming on earth the moral bent of his future life.

We may assume the same of men in similar conditions in Christian lands, men brought up amid ignorance and crime, men brought up in infidel homes, men to whom Christ has been so unattractively presented that they saw no beauty in Him or even instinctively turned away from Him impelled by their conscience. They all have the light of God in some degree and by their attitude towards the right that they know are determining on earth their attitude towards God in the Hereafter. They are forming character and *character tends to permanence.*

The "outer darkness" it would seem comes not from absence of light but from blindness of sight. The joy of Heaven is impossible to the unholy just as the joy of beautiful scenery to the blind or the joy of exquisite music to the deaf. Probation in this life—simply means that in this first stage of his being a man either is or is not blinding his eyes and dulling his ears and hardening his heart so as to make himself incapable of higher things in the life to come.

If then it be possible even for a heathen to have in this life sufficient probation to determine his attitude towards God for ever, how much more for a man in the full light of Christianity. In view of this the great law of life that CHARACTER TENDS TO PERMANENCE may it not be awfully true that a man who with full knowledge of Christ wilfully and deliberately turns from Him all through this life, should thus render himself incapable of turning to Him in any other life? *With full knowledge of Christ* I say, not with knowledge of some repulsive misrepresentation of Christ.

For think what it means to reject Christ wilfully with full knowledge of Him.

His voice still comes as we tramp on,
With a sorrowful fall in its pleading tone :
"Thou wilt tire in the dreary ways of sin ;
I left My home to bring thee in.
   In its golden street are no weary feet,
   Its rest is pleasant, its songs are sweet."
And we shout back angrily hurrying on
To a terrible home where rest is none :
"We want not your city's golden street,
Nor to hear its constant song !"
And still Christ keeps on loving us, loving all along.

Rejected still He pursues each one :
"My child, what more could thy God have
   done ?
Thy sin hid the light of heaven from Me,
When alone in the darkness I died for thee.
Thy sin of to-day in its shadow lay
Between My face and One turned away."
   And we stop and turn for a moment's space
   To fling back that love in the Saviour's face,

To give His heart yet another grief,
And glory in the wrong.
And still Christ keeps on loving us, loving all along.

Is it hard to believe that a man thus knowing Christ and wilfully rejecting Him should thereby risk the ruin of his soul? Can we not recognize this awful law of life that wilful sin against light tends to darkening of the light— that every rejection of God and good draws blood as it were on the spiritual retina, that a life of such rejections of the light tends to make one incapable of receiving the light for ever.

If this be so it is not at all fair to misrepresent it by saying that God cruelly stereotypes a man's soul at death and will refuse him permission to repent after death however much he may want to. The voice of the Holy Ghost within tells us that this could never be true of the Father. We must believe that through all Eternity, if the worst sinner felt touched by the love of God and wanted to turn to Him, that man would be saved. What we dread is that the man may not want to do so, may have rendered himself incapable of doing so. We dread not God's will, but the man's own will.

Character tends to permanence. Free will is

a glorious but a dangerous prerogative. All experience leads towards the belief that a human will may so distort itself as to grow incapable of good. Even a character not hardened into permanent evil may grow incapable of the highest good. A soul even forgiven through the mercy of God may "enter into life halt and maimed" like a consumptive patient cured of his disease but going through life with only one lung.

Though the Bible does not give an absolutely definite pronouncement on this question, yet the general trend of its teaching leads to the belief that this life is our probation time. It everywhere calls for immediate repentance. And St. Paul says that the Judgment is for deeds "done *in the body*," and there are such hints as "the door was shut" and "there is a sin unto death," and "it were better for a man not to have known the way of righteousness than after he has known it to turn from it." [1]   And this

---

[1] I have not quoted such texts as "Where the tree falleth there it shall lie," which no sensible student now uses in this connection, nor even the well-known text, "Behold now is the acceptable time, behold now is the day of salvation," for the

has been the general belief of the Church in all
ages. Even in all the hopeful words of the
ancient Fathers about Christ preaching to the
spirits in prison who in the dark old world days
" had sometime been disobedient," we have seen
that they add some such significant phrase as
" that He might convert those *who were capable*
of turning to Him. (See Chapter IV, p. 60.)
And human experience of character tending to
permanence makes this fact of human probation awfully probable. There is nothing in
Scripture nor in its interpretation by the Church,
nor in human experience, to conflict with the
statement that in this life Acts make habits and
Habits make Character and character makes
Destiny.

What new discoveries of God's power and
mercy may await us in eternity we cannot know,
but from all we do know we are justified in
thinking that (in the sense which I have stated)
a man's life in this world determines his destiny—at any rate that a man who presumes

"acceptable time" and "the day of salvation " mean here
not the present life of each man but the present Christian
dispensation. St. Paul is quoting Isaiah's prophecy of Christ
of the acceptable time and the day of salvation, and he says
this time has come now in this Christian dispensation.

recklessly on chances in the future is taking terrible risks. The Bible gives no encouragement to hope that one who with full knowledge of Christ keeps on wilfully rejecting Him all through this life will be able to turn to Him in any other life.

The only comfort we dare offer to anxious mourners grieving over sinful friends departed is that God only is the judge of what constitutes irrevocable rejection of good, that we cannot tell who has irrevocably " done despite to the Spirit of grace," and that the deep love and pain of Christ for sinful men remains for ever and ever. We may tell the poor mother that her deep love and pain for her dead son is but a faint shadow of the deep love and pain of God —that no one will be surprised or trapped in his ignorance—that no one will be lost whom it is possible for God to save—that no one will be lost until " the Heavenly Father has as it were thrown His arms around him and looked him full in the face with the bright eyes of His love, and that of his own deliberate will he would not have Him " (Faber).

We dare not minimize what the love and pain of God may do, but we dare not presume in the face of Scripture to lighten the awful responsibility which this life brings.

Thus we reach larger thoughts of God's dealings with man and deeper interest in the infinite variety that must be in the "many mansions" of the boundless life hereafter. And this sets us wondering about another thought as to ministry in that life.

CHAPTER XI

MINISTRY IN THE UNSEEN LIFE

§ 1

IS it allowable here to make a venture of faith and speculate on a matter of which we cannot give definite proof? There is a beautiful old allegory of KNOWLEDGE, the strong mailed knight, tramping over the great table-land that he surveyed, and testing and making his ground sure at every step, while beside him, just above the ground, moved the white-winged angel FAITH.

Side by side they moved, till the path broke short off on the verge of a vast precipice. Knowledge could go no further. There was no footing for the ponderous knight; but the white-winged angel rose majestically from the ground and moved across the chasm, where her companion could not follow.

Our path has broken off—knowledge can go no further. May we speculate with faith on something we cannot prove? I am thinking of a speculation very dear to myself, about that progress of our dear ones in the presence of Christ. Will not much of that progress in the life beyond come through unselfish ministry to others? Let us see what reason there is to hope it.

Think of all the true hearts who have lived on earth the Christ life of unselfish helpfulness. Can you imagine them never helping any one there, where growth in love is God's highest aim for them?

Think of our Lord's mysterious preaching in the Life after Death and remember that some of the best known teachers of the early Church believed that the apostles and others had followed His example.   (See Chapter IV, p. 59.)

Think that there are countless millions in the World of the Departed born in heathen lands, born in Christian lands, who had no chance on earth of knowing Christ in a way to win their love for Him.

Think, how shall His command be fulfilled by His Church, " Go preach the good news to every creature "—EVERY creature. What a mockery it seems with the heathen dying half a million every week if no work for Christ goes on in the Unseen! If millions of those Hindoos who have died without the Gospel would have accepted it, do you think it is not being taught to any of them now ? If the men of ancient Tyre and Sidon would have repented at the teaching and work of Christ, if the mighty works had been done in them, do you not think He has taken care since that the men of Tyre and Sidon should have their chance ? If the heathen Socrates, and Plato, and Marcus Aurelius, and Epictetus would have fallen at His feet as their Master and Friend—and you know they would—do you think they have not learned to know Him by now ? If honest hearts in our own land who have died repelled from Him through their ignorance and through stupid misrepresentations would have loved Him if they knew Him as He really is, do you think that no one is helping them to understand Him now ? Can we doubt that somehow within the Veil they will learn more fully of His tender love ? And judging from what we know of God's methods on earth, is it unreasonable to think that they will learn it from their brethren ? True, God might help them by means of the angels. But in God's dealings with men's souls on earth not angels but men were the helpers

He gave them.   Even in the stupendous miracle of the conversion of St. Paul it was a man (Ananias) whom God sent to help him.

§ 2

Here comes an interesting question about the doctrine of Election.   To the generation before us it was a horrible doctrine clashing with all sense of fairness or right.   Men said it meant that God decreed certain men to eternal Heaven and certain others to eternal Hell by His own arbitrary will.   The stern revolt of Conscience at length sent us back to study our Bibles more carefully.   We found that in the first recorded case of election Abraham was called *for the good of others* " that in thee and in thy seed shall all the families of the earth be blessed."

We saw reason to believe that Abraham's case was a type of all other elect—*elect for the service of others*.   We found that the Bible consistently and throughout affirms that when " God calls or separates one man to Himself it is for the good of other men; that when He selects one family it is that all families should be blessed; that when He chooses one nation it is for the welfare of all nations; that when He elects and establishes a church it is for the spiritual benefit of the world. No man, no family, no nation, no church possesses any gift or privilege or superior capacity or power for its own use and welfare alone but for the general good." So we learned that God's word is true in spite of our stupid misunderstanding of it and that this doctrine of Election rightly understood is one of the noblest things in the whole Bible.

Now comes my question. Are God's elect in the Hereafter life still "*elect for the service of others*"? Are those loving souls who are joyfully accepting Christ's service here,—destined for a still more glorious service in this ministry in the Unseen—the "first-fruits" of a great harvest which through them the Lord will reap in the Hereafter? Will some be just saved, saved so as by fire, saved "by the skin of their teeth," as we say, missing the noble destiny of the "elect," the joy of being a blessing to their race?

§ 3

"You have preached your last sermon," said one to Frederick Denison Maurice as he was dying. "Aye," he said; "but only my last sermon in THIS life." He believed he was going through the veil to preach to men. I believe it too, though I cannot prove it, nay, even though there be difficulties in the way of believing it. And many men greater than we are believing it, impelled by the stirring of Divine impulses within.

Do not think of it as merely a work for preachers and teachers. Every brave boy here who is trying to do right, every poor woman who is learning to love, every one who is blessing the world by kindly unselfishness, is helping on the Kingdom of God on earth and will be helping on the Kingdom of God beyond.

Surely there will be scope for them all. When you think of that great mingled crowd that is daily passing through the gates of death, all sorts and conditions—from the strong saints of God to the poor children brought up in homes of sin—you need have little doubt that there is room for service.

If it be true, ah! think of it, you who are trying to forget yourselves, and live for others —think of the blessedness of your life in the waiting land. With the weak and the ignorant needing to be helped; with the little children needing to be mothered and loved; with the great heathen world, who have gone within the veil, never yet having heard of Christ.

§4

If it be true, think how it takes away the reproach of "glorified selfishness," which many attribute to the Christians' glad hope.

Think how it helps in the perplexities about God's dealings when young and useful lives are taken from the earth. An angry mourner said to me recently, "I don't believe God has anything to do with it, else why should He take away a noble life like that and leave all these stupid useless people in the world?" I told him of my hope of this ministry in the Unseen and suggested that perhaps God did not want ONLY the stupid useless people.

And think especially how it deepens the importance of our life on earth to feel that it has a bearing on our usefulness for ever. The more we increase our talents here, the more we shall be able to help our Saviour there. He Himself suggests this in the parables of the Talents and the Pounds. "Thy pound has gained five, I

will set thee over five cities. Thy pound **has**
gained ten, I will set thee over ten cities. I
will give thee a larger and nobler work hereafter." Is not that an incentive to stir one's
blood ? The more I grow in love, in unselfishness, in knowledge of God, in righteousness of
life, the more use I shall be to **my dear Lord**
and to my brethren for ever.

CHAPTER XII

CONCLUSION

SO we close our thoughts about the NEAR HEREAFTER, the life immediately after death. The FAR Hereafter—the great mystery of Judgment and Hell and Heaven belongs to a later section. Here we have been dealing only with the life going on to-day in the Unseen—side by side with our present life.

Ah! that wonderful Paradise land—that wonderful Church of God in the Unseen—with its vast numbers, with its enthusiastic love, with all its grand leaders who have been trained on earth. WE AND THEY together form the great continuous Church of God. We are all ONE LONG PROCESSION; they at the head in the Unseen. What a life it is! What a work it has!

Said I not well it was a Gospel of the Hereafter, a good news of God! It will make you solemn as you feel that character passes on un-

changed. That is good ; but it will do more. It
will take away the sting and the horror of death.
It is not the pain of dying that makes that
horror when I come to die. After all, men
bear far more pain without flinching. It is not
merely the parting for the present with those I
love. We have constantly to do that when they
go to other lands without breaking our hearts
about it. It is not even any doubt about a
future Resurrection at the Second Advent. I
may believe that, and yet get little comfort
from it. That Advent seems so far away. It
may be next week ; but it may be 5,000 years
hence, and meantime what of my life ? Sleep,
unconsciousness, darkness ? What ? No wonder I should shrink from that mysterious unknown.

But teach me the ancient Scriptural doctrine
of the PARADISE life as it appears in the Bible.
Teach me that in the hour after death I shall
pass into the Unseen with myself, with my full
life, my feelings, my character, my individuality,
and in that solemn hour death will lose its
horror. Is not that a Gospel ?

In the awful days of bereavement it will
bring God's peace, and it will bring elevation

of character. "Where your treasure is, there
will your heart be also."

"He is not dead, the child of your affection,
  But gone into that school
Where he no longer needs your poor protection,
  And Christ Himself doth rule."

You think of your boy as serving at one side
of the veil, and you at the other; each in the
presence of Christ. You think how he is being
lovingly trained and disciplined. How all his
abilities are being used in self-sacrificing deeds
for others. Not in a glorified selfishness in
thanking God that he is safe, though his brethren be lost. Ah, no! but in perfect self-sacrifice, even as his Lord. You think of him as
learning to fight for righteousness—to help the
weak, aye, mayhap, to go out—God's brave
young knight—out into the darkness after some
one who has missed of Christ on earth. Realize
that and your whole life must perforce grow
nobler. And realize that you will not have to
wait for the Resurrection or the Advent to
meet him and learn all.

When your death comes, he will be waiting
for you. He has been praying and watching
over you. He will tell you of all that has been

happening. And together in Christ's loving presence, side by side, you will work and wait, and help your brethren; and look forward to the glory of the heaven that is still in the future. Is not that a Gospel worth the preaching —a Gospel to stir our souls and to comfort our hearts for those "whom we have loved long since and lost a while"?

Thank God for the blessed doctrine of the Paradise life!

Thank God for all His poor penitent servants departed this life in His faith and fear!

PART II

The Far Hereafter

I

THE JUDGMENT

WE touch lightly on the subject of the FAR Hereafter which is still away in the future for all humanity. One day the Intermediate Life will close. The end of this age will come at the Second Advent. And at this crisis our Lord places the great drama of the Judgment and the final decision of each man's destiny. Whether it will be a great spectacular event such as His picture suggests, with all humanity assembled and the Judge on the great White Throne, or whether His picture is figurative, we cannot affirm. We can only gather that it will be a final judgment and that it will be a judgment according to finally developed character, when men shall be clearly seen to belong to the right hand or the left, the sheep or the goats, to the wheat or the tares, to the good fish to be gathered up or the bad fish to be thrown away.

Then come the final stages in the history of humanity, Hell and Heaven.

II

HELL

HERE we touch the awful part of our study. In Christ's great drama of the Judgment those on the left hand are passing out into the darkness, and we see them no more. In that darkness there seems no ray of hope. So far as we can learn, it means irrevocable ruin and loss. In spite of God's love and pain for them on Earth and in Hades, they seem at last to have destroyed in themselves everything of good, and so placed themselves beyond possibility of restoration for ever. The judgment has clearly the ring of finality. There seems nothing more to be said. And so, with pain in our hearts responding to the pain of the Father, we are forced to leave them in the darkness and mystery in which Scripture enshrouds them.

This is, I think, all that can justifiably be said. The reticence and reserve of Scripture forbids any definite doctrine of Hell.

And this is all that would have needed to be

said if men had kept to that reticence and reserve of Scripture, and to all further questionings contented themselves with the answer that
the Judge of all the earth will do right. But
they have not so contented themselves. It is
hard to blame them. For beyond the main
facts about the doom of the impenitent there
are here and there through the Bible many tan-
talizing hints perplexing and difficult to reconcile with each other, but very tempting to follow out. By emphasizing certain of these and ignoring or dwelling more lightly on certain others
which seem to contradict them, men have for-
mulated definite doctrines about Hell, differing
widely from each other but each with apparently
strong Scriptural support. This is only what
may happen in any department of study. The
strict rule of evidence in any enquiry is that
all the facts must be studied and that no
theory shall be accepted as entirely trust-
worthy while any of the evidence remains
unaccounted for.

There are three theories which hold the
ground to-day, each of them seemingly with
much evidence in its favour, but each of them

seriously unsatisfactory as conflicting with other evidence.

(1) The theory of Everlasting Torment—that every soul which has missed ot Christ shall be plunged into a Hell of torment and sin for ever and ever, growing worse and worse and lower and lower through all the ages of Eternity.

(2) The theory of Universalism—that in the ages of the far future through the stern loving discipline of God all men shall at length be saved.

(3) The theory of Conditional Immortality —that all souls who fail of Eternal Life shall be punished not by Everlasting Torment, but by annihilation and the loss of God and Heaven for ever.

At first sight it seems almost impossible that such conflicting theories could be formed out of the same Bible. But a little consideration of the evidence and of the power of prejudice and preconceptions in estimating evidence makes it easier to understand.

The main trend of all Scripture teaching is that it shall be well, gloriously well, with the good, and that it shall be evil, unutterably evil, with the wicked. That there is a mysterious and awful malignity attaching to sin—that to be in sin means to be in misery and ruin in this life or any other life—and that sin persisted in tends to utter and irretrievable ruin. No arguments about the love and power of God to save to the uttermost can cancel the fact of the free-will of man or the plain statements of Scripture confirmed beyond question by the loving Lord Himself as to the awful fate of the finally impenitent.

But running through all this dark background of Scripture is a curious golden thread of prophecy that evil shall not be eternal in God's universe. One turns to it perplexed with wondering hope. For however fully Conscience recognizes the righteousness of a terrible retribution for sin, there is in all thoughtful minds a shrinking from the thought that Evil shall be as permanent as Good in the universe of the All-holy God—that any evil power can exist unendingly side by side with Him and unendingly resist Him; that Hell and Heaven, Satan and God shall co-exist for all eternity. This is almost unthinkable to thoughtful men. It is a Dualism repugnant to all our ideals of God. And this golden thread, running through the Old and New Testaments alike, confirms this thought, in its dim vision of a golden age somewhere away in the far future— away it would seem beyond the dark vision of Hell—when evil shall have vanished out of the Universe for ever and " God shall be all in all " (1 Cor. xv. 28)—when there shall come " the times of the Restoration of all things which God hath promised by the mouth of all His holy prophets since the world began" (Acts iii. 21).

Naturally there is danger of people emphasizing strongly either one of these trends of Scripture and gathering certain proof texts according to their own prejudices and preconceptions of what ought to be. " The way in which some people read their Bibles," says Mr. Ruskin, " is like the way in which the old monks thought that hedgehogs ate grapes. They rolled themselves over the grapes as they lay on the ground and whatever first stuck to their spikes they carried off and ate." If the grapes are of various kinds as are the passages of Scripture we cannot judge thus of the taste of the vintage.

To get the true taste of the grapes we must press them in cluster. To get the true meaning of Scripture we must study the whole trend of Scripture. Before we can accept any doctrine from separate passages of Scripture we must assure ourselves that it is in harmony, not only with other passages but also with the ruling thoughts which run through all Scripture, God's unutterable holiness, God's awful hatred of sin and stern denunciations of doom against the impenitent, God's love, God's unchangeableness, God's reasonableness and fairness, and the mysterious golden thread of hope which runs through all.

Now we glance as briefly as possible at the three theories referred to.

I

The theory of Everlasting Torment and Everlasting Sin.

This theory keeps with Scripture in asserting the fatal and irrevocable result of unrepented sin—but it goes beyond the reserve of Scripture in defining that result and so defining it as to impugn the character of God. It teaches that all who are condemned in the

Judgment are doomed to a life of endless torment, in the company of devils—forsaken of
God. Millions of millions of ages shall see this
punishment no whit nearer to its end. It must
go on for ever and ever and ever.

It takes perhaps a child's or a woman's heart
to realize the horror of that thought. I remember as a child reading a Sunday-school book that
helped me to realize the meaning of this " for
ever and ever in hell." I was to imagine a huge
forest, and a tiny insect coming from the farthest
planet and biting an atom out of one of the
leaves, and carrying it away to his home, the
journey taking one thousand years. Then I
was to imagine the ages that must elapse before
that whole leaf was carried off. Then the stupendous time before the whole tree would be
gone. Then, as my brain reeled at the thought,
I was to look forward to the carrying away of
the whole forest, and from that to the carrying
away of the whole world. Then came the awful sentence in italics, *Even then eternity would
but have begun.* I suppose God will forgive the
people who wrote that book for children if they
repent, but I don't feel much like forgiving
them. I can remember still lying awake in the

night and crying as I thought of the lost souls in Hell as my poor little brain reeled at the thought of the journeys of that wretched insect and of those whom God kept alive to suffer for ever and ever and ever.

Then as one grew older came the further horror that these "lost" are kept alive not only to suffer but to sin everlastingly. They are to go on increasing in sin for ever and ever and ever in the universe of the All-holy God. One tests this by the ruling thoughts of Scripture. One thinks of God's holiness. One thinks of the golden thread of hope. One wonders what it means that Christ came to "destroy the works of the devil"[1] and to destroy the devil (bruise the serpent's head[2]) and how one day "God shall be all in all" if straight opposite for all eternity shall be Satan's Kingdom of misery and sin. Surely Christ has not failed! And yet—and yet— what shall we say? And what shall we say of God's fatherhood? Shall we say as some do that as Judge He must do cruel things which as Father He would shrink from? God forbid! The Judge and the Father are one.

[1] 1 John iii. 8.   [2] Gen. iii. 15.

Men would never use such sophistry about the character of God if it were put into plain words. "Ye must ken," said a godly old Scotchman, "that the Almighty may often have to do in His offeeshial capacity what He would scorn to do as a private individual!" I quote this not with flippancy but with stern indignation. That is baldly what such sophistry means.

Clearly one who insists on this doctrine ought at least to be absolutely certain that Scripture leaves him no escape from it. Now the conclusion which a thorough study of the question leads to is this:—that Scripture nowhere definitely affirms that the sufferings of the lost *shall not be* everlasting, and nowhere definitely affirms that they *shall be* everlasting.

Even that if it be true is some relief. We should no longer be forced to believe of God what Conscience declares to be unworthy of Him. But is it true? I can already see the Bible turned over for the dark array of texts beginning with "He that believeth not shall be damned," "How can ye escape the damnation of Hell?" "These shall go away into everlasting punishment," etc.

Let me explain.

If we examine the Bible carefully we shall find that, while there are a great many clear proofs of the certainty and awfulness of Hell, the proofs of this theory of Everlasting Torment are not much to be depended on. Practically they can all be gathered into three groups.

In the first the chief word is DAMN or DAMNATION.

In the second the chief word is HELL.

In the third the chief word is EVERLASTING.

It is not too much to say that if these three sets of passages were removed from the Bible nobody would think of believing in everlasting torment. Now let me make the assertion straight out—There is no word in the original language of the Bible that at all justifies the use of either of these words in the meaning that we have attached to it—and therefore the Revised Version of the Bible has practically swept them all away.

§ 1

Take first the words Damn, Damnation which convey to us the idea of doom to a Hell of never-ending torment and never-ending sin.

The original word conveyed no such idea to our Lord or the Apostles. It conveyed no such idea to the translators of the Authorized Version. When they translated it Damn and Damnation they did not at all mean what we now mean.

There are two Greek words, κρίνω which means simply *to judge*, and κατα-κρίνω which means to *judge adversely*, to *condemn*, and it is sometimes the first and sometimes the second of these words which is translated "Damn." Why is it so translated? Surely the translators did not think so evil of God as to believe that He could never judge a man without condemning him and that He could never condemn him except to everlasting to.ment. Not at all. They had no thought of this. The English word "damn" at that time had no such awful meaning as has grown into it in our day through the wide-spread influence of the theory which I am criticizing. It simply meant what the Greek word meant. I find an interesting illustration of this in the Wycliffe Bible in the passage about the woman taken in adultery. Jesus saith, "Woman, hath no man damned thee?" "No man, Lord." "Neither do I

damn thee." That is to say the English word
Damn at that time only meant "*condemn.*"
But words are dangerous things if not carefully watched, owing to their tendency to
change their meaning as a language grows.
A new, darker meaning has grown on to the
English word since. Once an innocent word,
it has now become dangerous and misleading. Therefore, the Revisers have swept it
away, and *the words damn and damnation have
now vanished entirely and for ever out of the
pages of the English Bible.* Unfortunately the
public do not read the Revised Version.

With this explanation I ask the reader to
turn back to his Bible. In our sense of the
word did our Lord say, "He that believeth not
shall be damned"? Most certainly not. He
said that he should be *condemned* for wilfully
disbelieving, but He did not say to what he
should be condemned, nor for how long. I
should condemn you for doing a selfish act, but
that would hardly mean sending you to endless
torment. Did He say that those who had done
evil should rise to the resurrection of damnation? (1 John v. 29). No. He said, "to the

resurrection of judgment." (See R. V.) Did St. Paul say, " He that doubteth (about eating certain meats) is damned if he eat "? (Rom. xiv. 23). Did he say that a church widow should have damnation for marrying again? (1 Tim. v. 12). Of course not; the word only means judgment or condemnation. There is no thought at all in it of this endless Hell as the Revised Version has plainly shown. So we see that at any rate all these texts about "damnation" can no longer be used in proof of everlasting torment and everlasting sin.

§ 2

Something similar is true about the texts whose chief word is " Hell." The word " hell " occurs eighteen times in the Authorized Version. Once it is a translation of a Greek word Tartarus (2 Peter ii. 4) cast down to Hell to be reserved " *unto the Day of Judgment.*" That certainly was not everlasting. Five times it is a translation of the word Hades whose meaning we already know, and which certainly did not mean everlasting. The other twelve times it is a translation of the word Gehenna used by our Lord, and no scholar

with the least regard for his reputation would
dream of stating that our Lord certainly meant
it to convey the idea of endlessness. It was
the name of a horrible valley outside Jerusalem
where things were cast out to be burnt, to keep
the city pure. The Jewish prophets took the
word as a metaphor to express the fate of
wicked men. From it they drew their images
used by our Lord of " the worm that dieth not
and the fire that is not quenched " (Mark x. 46).
To be in danger of Gehenna was to be in
danger of a hereafter doom suggested by this
dread place.

Our Lord simply took up the vague Jewish
word and did not define it. What exactly had
He in His mind when He used this word?
This is a question of terrible importance. He
certainly meant something very stern and
awful. He seems to indicate also something
final and irrevocable. But there is absolutely
no reason to believe that He meant to convey
the idea in our minds of a vast prison, in
which the souls of the lost are pierced through
with agony for ever and ever. You ask, How
can I know what He meant? How could I
know what Shakespeare meant by a certain

word? I should read up all the books and letters of Shakespeare's times in which the word occurs, and whatever it commonly meant to the people of Shakespeare's time I should accept as being what Shakespeare meant. That looks sensible, does it not? Well, a very interesting investigation has been made by various scholars. They have examined all the existing Jewish writings where the word Gehenna was used from 300 B. C. to 300 A. D. Then they have examined the Jewish Talmuds which run on to the fourth and fifth century. A modern English scholar, Dr. Dewes, says (*Plea for a New Translation*, p. 23): "Every passage has been carefully examined which is quoted in the works of Lightfoot, Schoetgen, Buxtorf, Castell, Schindler, Glass, Bartoloccius, Ugalino and Nork, and the result of the whole examination is this: *there are only two passages which even a superficial reader could consider to be corroborative of the assertion that the Jews understood Gehenna to be a place of everlasting torment.*"

I give a few specimens from the Talmuds. "Gehenna is ordained of old because of sins." "The ungodly will be judged in Gehenna *against the day of judgment."* " The ungodly shall be judged in Gehenna *until the righteous shall say of them, We have seen enough."* " The judgment of the ungodly is for twelve months." "Gehenna is nothing but a day in which the impious will be burned." " The sinners . . . shall descend into Gehenna ; at the end of twelve months the body shall be consumed and the soul burned up and the wind shall scatter it under the feet of the just."

The reader sees, of course, that the vague Jewish opinions have no authority for us except to help us to get at the meaning of our Lord when speaking to Jews about Gehenna. We may assume that He used their familiar word in the sense in which they would naturally understand it. They certainly would understand Him to proclaim some terrible doom, probably also an irrevocable doom. But can any one affirm that they must have understood Him to mean endless torment, in the face of this evidence—and its powerful confirmation by the greatest of all modern Jewish students of the Talmud, Emanuel Deutsch. " There is no everlasting damnation in the Talmud " (*Remains*, p. 53), and again, " There is not a word in the

Talmud which supports the damnable dogma of endless torment" (Conversation with Mr. Cox, *Salvator Mundi*, p. 72).

The American Revised Version has very wisely removed the word Hell altogether on account of the misleading associations connected with it. It substitutes the word Gehenna, leaving the reader to ascertain its meaning. The English Revisers have retained the word Hell and put the word Gehenna beside it in the margin. I think this was a pity, as it will be hard for the ordinary reader to dissociate the word Hell from the theory which has unwarrantably grown on to it. But at any rate I think we may safely say that no reader who understands the position will ever again use the texts in which our Lord speaks of Hell to prove the absolute certainty of the theory of Endless Torment and Endless Sin. So vanishes another group of the proof texts for this theory.

§ 3

Now take the group of texts with the word "everlasting." It is surely significant that the Revisers have completely removed this word also in every case and substituted for it the word "eternal," a less definite word and which in scholarly usage means rather the opposite of temporal—that which is above the sphere of time and space—that which belongs to the other world. At any rate the fact that they have removed it in every case shows that the word "everlasting" did not seem to them a correct translation.

There is only space for a brief explanation. The original word is the adjective αἰώνιος (aionios) (Eng. æonian), coming from the noun αἰών (aion) (Eng. æon), an age, an epoch, a long period of time. This noun cannot mean eternity for it is repeatedly used by St. Paul in the plural "æons" and "æons of æons." As we speak of great periods of time, "the Ice Age," "the Stone Age," etc., so the Bible speaks of "this age" (æon), "the coming age" (æon), and "the end of the age," etc. These æons or ages are thought of in Scripture as vast periods past, present and future in which the Divine purpose is working itself out, *e. g.*, God's purpose is the purpose of the ages (æons) (Eph. iii. 11). Christ's name is above every name not only in this age (æon) but in that which is to come

(Eph. i. 21). "That in the ages (æons) to come
He might shew," etc.

From this noun, then, comes the adjective
αἰώνιος (aionios)—æonian which may be defined
"age long " or "belonging to the ages," etc.
Any Greek scholar will assert unhesitatingly
that of itself it does not mean endless or everlasting. Sometimes, as when applied to God,
it may be thus translated but only because the
meaning is inherent in the noun to which it is
applied. The word *αἰώνιος* of itself would not
positively prove the endlessness of God. This
adjective when applied to any thing or any
state of being cannot of itself be used to prove
its endlessness.

It is worth notice too that in the Septuagint
Greek Bible, the version usually quoted in the
Gospels and Epistles, this word *αἰώνιος* is fre-
quently applied to things that have ended, *e. g.*,
the gift of the land of Canaan, the priesthood of
Aaron, the kingdom of David, the temple at Jerusalem, the daily offerings, etc. When the noun
always means a finite period and the adjective is
applied both to that which is ended and to that
which is endless it would surely be poor scholar-
ship if the Revisers allowed the word "ever-

lasting " to remain as its translation, or if students of theology should argue from it the endlessness of anything. To which we may add that there are Greek adjectives and phrases which *do definitely mean* " endless " and which are never used in the Bible of men's fate in the Hereafter.

Be it observed that all this does not prove that the punishment of the future ages *may not* be everlasting. It only proves that Scripture nowhere asserts unmistakably that *it must be so*. It simply asserts that it is æonian.

The thoughtful advocates of Everlasting Torment are of course aware of all this. But they honestly feel that in spite of the indefiniteness of the adjective, our Lord has fixed His meaning beyond question in the one passage that has become so famous as the great proof text in this controversy, " These shall go away into *æonian* punishment, but the righteous into *æonian* life " (Matt. xxv. 46). Very reasonably they say, " If the word asserts everlastingness in the one case it must also in the other." The answer is that the word *of itself* cannot assert everlastingness in either case. If this word were our only proof of everlasting life then everlasting life would be a doubtful matter. But the everlastingness of that life like the everlastingness of God is evident all over the Bible quite apart from this. The words here simply tell that the one shall go into the æonian life and the other into æonian punishment, *i. e.*, that the one shall go into the life of the future age and the other into the punishment of the future age without exactly specifying the duration of either.

I quite feel that the close connection of the words suggests at least the probability that one is as lasting as the other. Yet even that consideration is weakened by asking if people are willing to apply it to St. Paul's statement, "As in Adam *all* die even so in Christ shall *all* be made alive" (the context suggests eternal life). I would point out, too, that a somewhat similar verse is in the Septuagint Bible of our Lord's day in Hab. iii. 6, where the (æonian) everlasting mountains were scattered before God, whose ways are (æonian) everlasting. Yet it does not prove that the one is as endless as the other. And in Rom. xvi. 25–26 the mystery hid in the (æonian) times "before the world began" is now manifested according to the

command of the (æonian) eternal God. But
the age " before the world began " is ended.

At any rate I must leave the matter here.
I have no space for fuller statement. If any
man feels that a world of increasing sin and
awful torment growing no nearer to its end
after millions and millions of ages does not dis-
turb his conscience or the thoughts of God
which he has learned from the whole trend of
Scripture this text will probably weigh strongly
with him in spite of all that I have said. But
to him who is tortured by such a thought of God
and yet feels that Scripture binds him to it, it
must surely be some relief to feel that even in
this great bulwark text of Everlasting Torment
our Lord only asserts that these shall go away
into the æonian punishment or chastisement[1]
whatever that may mean.

Reluctantly, impelled by a sense of duty, I
have dealt with this theory more fully than
with the others. Should any godly people fear
that I am lightening an awful deterrent to

[1] κόλασις—chastisement, correction, punishment (see
Greek Lexicon).

sin let me say what long experience has taught me of the danger of this common theory.

It is making sad loving hearts whom God has not made sad and making earnest Christians, who feel forced to believe it, perplexed about the love and justice of God and the prophecies of the final victory of good.

It is forcing into the background the true and awfully solemn teaching about Hell which ought to be prominent in all our pulpits. When men cannot see any possible reconciliation between the doctrine of God's love and their doctrine of Hell they are very apt to find an easy way out. "We cannot reconcile them," said a young layman to me one day, "therefore we drop out one of them—Hell." Do not be shocked at it. Many besides my young layman are unconsciously doing it. Nowadays more than ever we, clergy, are teaching much about the love of God. But nowadays more than ever we are holding our tongues about Hell. We know the horrible idea which Hell commonly conveys. Therefore we keep it in the background trusting that our hearers will leave it there during the sermon on God's love. But they do not, and so we are very unconvincing about both doctrines.

Again, this common theory of Hell is so un-reasonable that it has lost its power as a deterrent. No teaching from which Conscience revolts can long hold its power over men. The rough common sense, the rough moral sense of careless men makes them reject it and treat it as a subject of jest. When men can stupidly laugh together over jests about hell-fire, when the devil is presented as a clown in the panto-mime it indicates something very wrong in the teaching. No doctrine has any real hold on the crowd when they can lightly jest about it. And because of their unbelief in this false notion of Hell they are ceasing to believe in any Hell at all—ceasing to believe in that awful real Hell which is taught in the Bible and of which God is giving some men foretastes even in this life.

And this false notion of Hell tends to shake men's belief in the reality of Heaven. For if the redeemed could enjoy their bliss in Heaven, knowing that myriads are ex-isting for ever and ever in endless suffering and still worse in endless sin, one feels that they have grown so selfish and opposite to Christ that they have no business in any heaven.

We dare not leave out the love of God and we dare not leave out the doctrine of Hell. Both are certainly true. Therefore they must be capable of reconciliation. The reconciliation must not come in ignoring Hell or believing in a kindly, good-natured God who does not judge severely about moral character and who only cares that His child should stop crying and be happy. We are having too much of this sentimentalism nowadays. It is a miserable misconception of that awful holiness which is "of purer eyes than to behold inquity." It would never explain the need of Christ dying on the cross to put away sin.

Whatever reconciliation we find here or hereafter it must have at bottom God's unutterable hatred of sin but also God's unutterable love and pain over every sinful soul which He has made. This theory of Endless Torment and Endless Sin certainly does not appear to satisfy this test, and it has in addition to face the stern revolt of Reason and Conscience.

II

The theory of Universalism, i. e., that all men shall at length be saved.

This opinion is based on the more hopeful side of Scripture that we have referred to, but it ignores or explains away what contradicts it in the darker and sterner side. If one could forget that, it would be the most inspiring of all the guesses that have been made. As presented by its best exponents, such men as Allen and Jukes and Cox, it is wonderfully attractive and at first sight seems to satisfy many of the conditions of the problem. It takes account of a just and awful retribution for every sin, and takes account also of the mysterious hope in the Hereafter which runs through the Bible. It believes that the power of God has infinite resources and that the love of God has unwearying persistence and that no soul can ultimately resist such resources and such love. Even Hell itself it deems God's final effort when all other means have failed.

The reader who thinks there can be no possible excuse for such a theory should glance at a few of the passages quoted in its favour:

"God who wills that *all men* should be saved"

(1 Tim. ii. 4), and "who wills that *all men*
should come to repentance" (2 Peter iii. 9).
And this will or determination of God is "*im-
mutable*" (Heb. vi. 7). Again, "Now is the
judgment of this world, now shall the Prince
of this world be cast out, AND I, if I be lifted up,
will draw *all men* unto Myself" (John xii. 31, 32).
"*All flesh* shall see the salvation of God"
(Luke iii. 6). "His grace bringing salvation to
all men" (Titus ii. 11). "We trust in the living
God who is the Saviour of *all men, especially*
of those who believe" (1 Tim. iv. 10). "He is
the propitiation *not for our sins only, but also*
for the sins of the *whole world*" (1 John ii. 2).
"He was manifested that He might *destroy* the
works of the devil" (1 John iii. 8) [and *destroy*
the devil (bruise the serpent's head) Gen.
iii. 15]. "He shall *overcome* the strong man
armed (the devil) and take away his armour
and divide his spoils" (Luke xi. 21, 22). "He
was manifested to *put away* sin by the sacrifice
of Himself" (Heb. ix. 26). "God hath not cast
away His people whom He foreknew . . .
and so *all Israel shall be saved*" (Rom. xii. 25–33).
"The times of the *Restoration of all things*
which God hath promised by the mouth of all

His holy prophets since the world began"
(Acts iii. 21). "As in Adam *all* die, even so in
Christ shall *all* be made alive. But every man
in his own order : Christ the first-fruits ; afterwards they that are Christ's at His coming.
Then cometh the end . . . when all things
have been *subjected unto Him* [1] . . . then
shall the Son also be *subjected unto Him* that
put all things under Him that God may be all
in all " (1 Cor. xv. 22–29).

One can see how the constant study of such
passages should lead men to an enthusiastic
hope and lead them to study less carefully the
stream of darker teaching that seemed to conflict with these. Whatever may be said against
the advocates of Universalism we at least owe
to them a clearer emphasizing of the mysterious
hopefulness of Scripture as to the final triumph
of good.

But with deep reluctance one is bound to assert that the advocates of Universal Salvation
to a great degree ignore or explain away unsat-
isfactorily much of the sterner side of the

---

[1] The same Greek words are used of His enemies' subjection to Christ as of Christ's subjection to the Father sug-
gesting that it would be of the same kind.

Bible. For amid all its hopefulness there is a steadily persistent note in Scripture, stern, awful, sorrowful, which seems impossible to reconcile with Universalism. There are clear and repeated assertions that some men at any rate will not be saved. It is St. Paul, the author of so many of those hopeful Scriptures quoted, who tells us " even weeping " of men " whose end is destruction " (Phil. iii. 19), and of those whose fate shall be " eternal destruction from the presence of God " (2 Thess. i. 9). It is the loving Christ Himself who said of one of His apostles, " It were good for that man if he had not been born " (St. Matt. xxvi. 24).

We are warned back too by the tendency of character to grow permanent. And when we are told that God " willeth all men to be saved," and that God can do everything, we are forced to ask, Can God do contradictory things ? Can God make a door to be open and shut at the same time ? Can God make a thing to be and not to be at the same time ? Can God make a man's will free to choose good or evil and yet secure that he shall certainly choose good at the last ? One longs to believe that Universalism should be true, but to believe it we must ignore much of the evidence of Scripture.

III

The theory of Conditional Immortality, *i. e.,* that all souls who fail of Eternal Life shall be punished not by Endless Torment, but by Annihilation and the loss of God and Heaven for ever and ever.

This is another conjecture framed to escape the difficulties of the former two. It would be consistent both with retribution for evil and also with the final victory of good. That in the mysterious nature of things when the malignity of sin becomes incurable, a soul rotted through with sin might ultimately die out of existence; this opinion is at least allowable as a conjecture to escape from the theory of Endless Torment and Sin. It would in a real sense be an everlasting punishment, being an everlasting loss of Heaven and God. But it too is founded only on part of the evidence, on such texts as " The gift of God is eternal life," " He that hath the Son hath life," implying that immortality is a conditional thing granted only to those who are saved, and such texts as " eternal *destruc-*

tion from the presence of God," and the idea
of utter annihilation in such passages as "burn
up the chaff with unquenchable fire." There
is much in favor of it but there is much in
Scripture which makes it difficult to accept
it. And it contradicts straight out the wide-
spread Christian belief in the essential immortality of the soul (though that belief also needs
to be examined). At any rate it cannot claim
authority as a theory of future punishment.

IV

These are the only conjectures offered us to
solve the difficulties connected with Final Retribution. We find them all unsatisfactory.
We have reached no definite doctrine of Hell.
With the evidence at our disposal it seems impossible to do so. The failure of all attempts
at reconciling the seeming contradictions of
Scripture must suggest to us that the solution
of this problem is beyond the range of our
present powers. At any rate it is beyond the
range of our present knowledge. Surely it is
wise and reverent to think that this points to
some dealing of God beyond our human ken
which will one day reconcile all the difficul

ties.[1] Our little guesses do not exhaust God's possibilities. Some day we shall find the answer in that land where we shall know even as we are known. And when we find it we know it will be consistent with our highest thoughts of God. I like to think that it is those who have grown closest to Christ in sympathy for sorrow and pain and who unlike us, know all the facts of the case, who are represented as joining in that glad shout hereafter, "Hallelujah! salvation and glory and power belong to our God, FOR TRUE AND RIGHTEOUS ARE HIS JUDGMENTS." Leave the manifestation of this to God. A wise old man once said, "God has a good deal of time to do things between this and the other side of eternity."

This then is the conclusion of the whole matter. A return to the reserve and reticence of Scripture. But with this result of our study, that we feel no longer forced to believe of God that which Conscience declares to be unworthy of Him. We are set free to believe that the Judge of all the earth will do right—that

---

[1] In other antinomies of Scripture, e. g., Man's free will and God's foreknowledge, we have to take refuge in a similar belief.

Hell as well as Heaven is within the confines
of His dominion—that evil shall not last for
ever; that in spite of all its conflicting evidence the trend of Scripture moves towards the
golden age, the final victory of good.

Thus we leave it.

In our final vision of humanity in Christ's
great drama of the Judgment, those on the left
are passing into the outer darkness and as they
pass the curtain falls behind them and we
see them no more. We know not what is passing in that outer darkness where there is
"weeping and gnashing of teeth." We have
no grounds to believe that any soul there is
being born again through sorrow and shame,
that any spoiled and deformed life is being re-
moulded in that awful crucible of God.

But as we watch the awful shadows of that
outer darkness, there comes beyond it on the
far horizon the quivering of a coming dawn.
For that age of God's Gehenna is to have its
end, and far away the day will dawn for which
the whole creation groaneth and travaileth together; when evil shall have vanished out of
the universe for ever; when death and Hell,
the evil and the Evil One shall be cast into the

lake of fire; when "at the name of Jesus every knee shall bow of things in Heaven and earth, and under the earth" (in the world of the dead). "And every tongue shall confess that Jesus Christ is Lord to the glory of God the Father." "Then cometh the end," says St. Paul, "when Christ shall deliver up the Kingdom to God, even the Father, when all His enemies shall be subjected unto Him. And when all His enemies have been subjected unto Him, then shall the Son also Himself be subjected unto Him that put all things under Him, that God may be all in all."

That is what shall be. One day, somewhere in the far mysterious future the "purpose of the ages" shall be accomplished. Evil shall have vanished out of the universe for ever and God shall be all in all. One day again it shall be as at the creation when "God looked on everything that He had made and behold it was very good." How? We know not and we need not know. We need not be able to assert dogmatically how He will accomplish His purpose. We need not be able to assert that all men shall be saved or that all who are not will be annihilated. But we must be able with trustful hearts to assert God's love and God's power and the final abolishing of evil, even though we can only do it with the poet's vagueness:

At last I heard a voice upon the slope
Cry to the summit, "Is there any hope?"
To which an answer pealed from that high land,
But in a tongue no man could understand,
And on the glimmering summit far withdrawn
God made Himself an awful rose of dawn.

III

HEAVEN

AT last " I " has reached the goal. In that far future comes the glad *finale* of human history, the realization of the eternal thought in the mind of God from the beginning. As the unwritten play of a great dramatist lies in his mind before it is uttered or acted, with every problem solved and every contingency provided for—so we believe the whole extended drama lay in the Eternal Mind—the path of struggle and pain —the cross-currents of human will—the glorious conclusion of it all. Nothing was an after-thought. Now at last Christ "shall see of the travail of His soul and shall be satisfied." Aye —satisfied. It was worth the cost. Worth the Incarnation of the Eternal Son—worth the sorrow and the pain—worth being misunderstood and shamed and mocked and scourged and spitted on and crucified—this final satisfaction of His tender love. " Eye hath not seen nor ear heard nor hath it entered into the heart of man to conceive the things that God

199

hath prepared. They shall hunger no more nor thirst any more, neither shall the sun light on them nor any burning heat, for the Lamb which is in the midst of the Throne shall shepherd them and lead them to eternal fountains of waters, and God shall wipe away every tear from their eyes. There shall be no more death—no mourning nor crying nor pain any more, for the former things—the old bad things —have passed away." That is the end of God's purpose for men. Surely it will be the wondering cry of the angels for ever, " Behold how He loved them ! "

I. WHAT IS MEANT BY HEAVEN?

To us with our limited faculties Heaven is practically inconceivable. We have no experience that would help us to realize it. Even the inspired writers can but touch the thought vaguely in allegory and gorgeous vision, piling up images of earthly things precious and beautiful—thrones and crowns and gates of pearl and golden streets in the heavenly city "coming down from God prepared as a bride adorned for her husband."

The only clear thought we have about

external things in Heaven is that "I" who lived here in an earthly body and in the Near Hereafter lived a spirit life "absent from the body" — shall in that Far Hereafter have a spiritual body analogous we suppose to the body "I" had on earth. Not the poor body, certainly, which rotted in the grave, "ashes to ashes, dust to dust" but a "glorified body," and yet it would seem having some strange mysterious connection with the earthly body. As the oak is the resurrection body of the acorn, and the lily of the ugly little bulb that decayed in the ground, "so also is the resurrection of the dead. It is sown in corruption, it is raised in incorruption; it is sown in weakness, it is raised in power; it is sown a natural body, it is raised a spiritual body." That gives very little information but it gives some tangible idea to grasp. Beyond this there is no hold for imagination.

But as we saw in the earlier chapters on the Intermediate Life I am still "I," the same conscious self through the whole life of Earth and Hades and Heaven, and therefore the *real life, the inner life* can still be understood. So when we enquire what can be known about the meaning of Heaven—at the very start I strike the key-note of the thoughts that follow, in the words of Christ Himself, " The Kingdom of God is within you." Heaven is a something within you rather than without you. Heaven means character rather than possessions. The Kingdom of God is not meat and drink, but Righteousness and Peace and Joy in the Holy Ghost.

That is the thought which I am trying to keep prominent all through this book. Hades life is dependent on character. Judgment is a sorting according to character. Heaven and Hell are tempers or conditions of character within us. They are not merely places to which God sends us arbitrarily. They are conditions which we make for ourselves. If God could send all men to Heaven, all men would be there. If God could keep all men from Hell, no one would be there. It is character that makes Heaven. It is character that makes Hell. They are states of mind that begin here, and are continued and developed there.

I have known men who were in Hell here— they told me so—men of brutal character, men

in delirium tremens, who saw devils grinning at
them from the bed. That if continued and developed would mean Hell there. I have known
sweet, unselfish lives who are in Heaven here.
That continued and developed would mean
Heaven there. You know how one could be in
Heaven here. Do you remember these wonderful words of our Lord, " No man hath ascended
into Heaven, only the Son of Man who is in
Heaven " ? Not *was*, not *shall be*, but *is* always
in Heaven, because always in unselfish love—
always in accord and in communion with God.
So, you see, a man carries the beginning of
Heaven and Hell within him, according to the
state of his own heart. A selfish, godless man
cannot have any Heaven so long as he remains
selfish and godless. For Heaven consists in
forgetting self, and loving God and man with
heart and soul.

§ 2

Do you see, then, the mistake that people
have been making in discussing what is meant
by Heaven? In all ages—in all races—men
have speculated about it, and their speculations
have been largely coloured by their characters

and temperaments. The Indian placed it in
the Happy Hunting Ground. The Greeks
placed it in the Islands of the Blest, where
warriors rested after the battle. The North-
man and the Mussulman had his equally sensual
Heaven. And many Christians have as foolish
notions as any one else. Some think that they
win Heaven by believing something with their
minds about our Lord's atonement. Some
think they go to Heaven by soaring up through
the air. Some of them, taking in its literal
meaning the glorious imagery of the Apocalypse, picture to themselves streets of beaten
gold and walls of flashing emerald and jasper,
and the wearing of crowns and the singing of
Psalms over and over again through all the
ages of eternity.

What is the fault in all such? That they do
not understand what Heaven really means.
They think of it as a something outside them
which anybody could enjoy if he could only
get there. They do not understand that Heaven
means the joy of being in union with God—that
the outward Heaven has no meaning till the inward Heaven has begun in ourselves. I need
not point out to you that our immortal spirits

would find little happiness in golden pave-
ments and gates of pearl. People on this
earth, who have their fill of gold and pearl, do
not always gain much happiness from them.
They are mere external things—they cannot
give eternal joy, because that comes from
within, not from without. It depends not on
what we have, but on what we are, not on the
riches of our possessions, but on the beauty of
our lives.

The gorgeous vision of the Apocalypse has
its meaning, but it is not the carnal, literal
meaning of foolish men. It tells of the bright
river of the water of life; of glorified cities,
where nothing foul, or mean, or ignoble shall
dwell; of the white robes of our stainless
purity; of the crowns and palms, the emblems
of victory over temptation; of the throne
which indicates calm mastery over sin; of the
song and music and gladsome feasting to image
faintly the abounding happiness and the fervent
thanksgiving for the goodness of God. They
are all mere symbols—mere earthly pictures
with a heavenly meaning, and the meaning
which lies behind them all is this: *The joy of
Heaven means the inward joy; the joy of char-*

acter ; the joy of goodness ; the joy of likeness to the Nature of God. That is the highest joy of all—the only joy worthy of making Heaven for men who are made in the image of God.

§ 3

It is not difficult to show this to any true man or woman who is humbly trying to do beautiful deeds on earth. Of course, if a man be very selfish and worldly ; a man who never tries to help another ; a man who smiles at these things as unreal sentiment ; who tells you that hard cash and success in life, and " to mind number one," as they say, are the chief things ; a man who never feels his pulses beat faster at the story of noble deeds—you cannot absolutely prove to him that the joy of char- acter is the highest happiness. You cannot prove to a blind man the beauty of the sunset sky ; you cannot arouse a deaf man to enthu- siasm about sweet music ; and you cannot prove to an utterly selfish, earthly man that self-sacrifice and purity and heroism and love are the loveliest and the most desirable pos- sessions—the sources of the highest and most lasting joy. But I feel sure that most of us, with all our faults, have in our better moments the desire and the admiration—aye, and the effort, too, after nobleness of life, and therefore we can understand this highest joy of Heaven. We have had experience sometimes, however rarely, of lovely deeds, and the sweet, pure joy that follows in their train. Well, whenever you have conquered some craving temptation or borne trouble for another's sake ; when you have helped and brightened some poor life, and kept quiet in the shade that no one should know of it ; when you have tried to do the right at heavy cost to yourself ; when the old father or mother at home has thanked God for the comfort you have been in their declining years ; whenever in the midst of all your sins you have done anything for the love of God or man, do you not know what a sweet, pure happiness has welled up in your heart, entirely different in kind, infinitely higher in degree than any pleasure that ever came to you from riches or amusement or the applause of men. Of this kind surely must be the pure joy of Heaven. Call up the recollection of some of those cherished moments of your life, and multiply by infinity the pleasure that you felt, and you will have some faint notion of what is meant by Heaven, the Heaven that God designs for man.

II. WHAT IS HEAVEN'S SUPREME JOY?

Thus, then, we answer the first of our questions—What is meant by Heaven? Heaven means a state of character rather than a place of residence. Heaven means to be something rather than to go somewhere. But though Heaven means a state of character rather than a place of residence, yet it means a place of residence, too. And though Heaven means to be something rather than to go somewhere, yet it means to go somewhere, too. And from this the second question easily follows. What can be known about that life in Heaven?

" Oh, for a nearer insight into Heaven,
  More knowledge of the glory and the joy,
Which there unto the happy souls is given,
  Their intercourse, their worship, their em-
    ploy."

We do not know a great deal about it.
The Bible is given to help us to live rightly

in this world, not to satisfy curiosity about the other world. But yet some glimpses of the blessed life have come to us, for our teaching.

The first thing to learn is that the chief joy of Heaven shall consist in that of which we can only dream in this life, of which we can have but a partial glimpse even in the Hades or Paradise Life—*the Beatific Vision*, the clear vision and knowledge of God. All this life and all the Paradise life are fitting and training and preparing us for this consummation.

Wise theologians of old divided the happiness of Heaven into "*Essential*" and "*Accidental.*" By *essential* they meant the happiness which the soul derives immediately from God's presence, from the Beatific Vision. By *accidental* they meant the additional happiness which comes from creatures, from meeting with friends, from the joyous occupations and all the delights of ever-widening knowledge.

But the Presence of God, the Vision of God, is the essential thing which gives light and joy to all the others. Without that Vision of God all would be dark as this beautiful world would be without the sun. Without that joy of God's presence all other joys would be spoiled, just as the gifts of this life would be without the central gift of health.

That is the central thought about Heaven in the Bible, the central thought of God's noblest saints of old, aye, and the central thought of some of the noblest amongst ourselves to-day.

Does it seem unreal, unnatural, to some of us ? I can well believe it. Few of us love God well enough yet to desire Him above all things. Most of us, I fear, if we would honestly confess it, think more of the joy of meeting our dear ones than of the joy of being with God. But God is very gentle with us. "He knoweth our frame ; He remembereth that we are but dust." He will gradually train us here and hereafter, and one day we, too, shall love Him above all things. Oh! I do think that to know the tender patience of Christ's love as we shall know it then, to know God as He is, with all the false notions about Him swept away, will make it impossible to withhold our love from Him. And if even our poor love for each other on earth is such a happiness think what joy may come from dwelling in that unutterable Love of God.

III. The Life in Heaven

What can we know further about the life in Heaven, about what the old theologians called the *secondary* or *accidental* joys as compared with the supreme joy of the Beatific Vision ?

We know, first, *There shall be no sin there.* It shall be a pure and innocent life. All who on earth have been loving, and pure, and noble, and brave, and self-sacrificing, shall be there. All who have been cleansed by the blood of Christ from the defilements of sin, and strengthened by the power of Christ against the enticements of sin, shall be there. There shall be no drunkenness nor impurity there, nor hatred, nor emulation, nor ill temper, nor selfishness, nor meanness. Ah! it is worth hoping for. We poor strugglers who hate ourselves and are so dissatisfied with ourselves, who look from afar at the lovely ideals rising within us, who think sorrowfully of all which we might have been and have not been—let us keep up heart. One day the ideal shall become the real. One day we shall have all these things for which God has put the craving in our hearts to-day. We shall have no sin there. We shall desire only and do only what is good. We shall be there

what we have only seemed or wished to be
here—honest, true, noble, sincere, genuine to
the very centre of our being.

No sin there.

§ 2

And   that will make it easier to under
stand the second fact revealed to us. *No sorrow there.* " They shall hunger no more,
neither thirst any more.   There shall be no
more curse . . .   no pain, nor sorrow, nor
crying, and God shall wipe away all tears from
their eyes." That is not hard to believe. Sin
is the chief cause of our sorrow on earth. If
there be no sin there; if all are pure and unselfish and generous and true, and if God wipes
away all tears that come from causes other than
sin, it is easily understood.

But let us not degrade this thought or make
it selfish or unreal.   One often hears the sneer
or the doubt about the happiness of Heaven
while any exist who have lost their Heaven.
We do not know the answer now.   But we shall
know it then.   And we must be absolutely certain that the answer lies not in the direction of
selfish indifference.   The higher any soul on

earth grows in love the less can it escape unselfish sorrow for others. Must it not be so in
that land too? Surely the Highest Himself
must have more pain than any one else for the
self-caused misery of men. If there be joy in
His presence over one that repenteth must there
not be pain over one that repenteth not? We
can only say in our deep ignorance that until
the day when all evil shall have vanished there
are surely higher things in God's plan for His
redeemed than selfish happiness and content.
There is the blessedness that comes of sympathy
with Him in the pain which is the underside of
the Eternal Love.

§ 3

No sin in Heaven. No sorrow in Heaven.
What else do we certainly know? *That the
essence of the Heaven life will be love.* The giving of oneself for the service of others. The
going out of oneself in sympathy with others.
There at last will be realized St. Paul's glorious
ideal. There it can be said of every man, He
suffereth long and is kind; envieth not; vaunteth
not himself; is not puffed up; seeketh not his
own; behaveth not uncourteously. He is like

the eternal God Himself, who beareth all
things, hopeth all things, endureth all things
(1 Cor. xiii. 4–7).

§4

We may well believe *that there will be no dead
level of attainment,* no dead level of perfection
and joy. That would seem to us very uninter-
esting. If we may judge from God's dealings
here and from the many texts of Scripture, there
will be an infinite variety of attainment, of
positions, of character. " In the Father's house
there are many mansions." Our Lord assumes
that we would expect that from our experience
here. "If it were not so, I would have told
you." I suppose there will be little ones there
needing to be taught and weak ones needing to
be helped ; strong leaders sitting at His right
hand in His Kingdom, and poor backward ones
who never expected to get into it at all.

And so surely we may believe, too, will there
be *varieties of character and temperament.* We
shall not lose our identity and our peculiar
characteristics by going to Heaven, by being
lifted to a higher spiritual condition. Just as
a careless man does not lose his identity by

conversion, by rising to a higher spiritual state
on earth, so we may well believe when we die
and pass into the life of the waiting souls, and
again when at Christ's coming we pass into the
higher Heaven we shall remain the same men
and women as we were before and yet become
very different men and women. Our lives will
not be broken in two, but transfigured. We
shall not lose our identity; we shall still be
ourselves; we shall preserve the traits of character that individualize us; but all these personal traits and characteristics will be suffused
and glorified by the lifting up of our motive
and aim. As far as we can judge, there will
be a delightful, infinite variety in the Heaven-
life.

§ 5

What else? There shall be *work in Heaven*.
The gift of God is eternal *life* and that life
surely means activity. We are told " His servants shall serve Him." We are told of the man
who increased the talents or the pounds to five
or ten that he was to be used for glorious work
according as he had fitted himself—" Lord, thy
talent hath gained five talents, ten talents."

What was the reply? "You are now to go and rest for all eternity." Not a bit of it. "Be thou ruler over five cities, over ten cities; enter thou into the joy of thy Lord." I know some men who are now retired after a very busy active life of work, and they hate the idleness, they are sick of it. No wonder the conventional Heaven does not appeal to them. Ah, that is not God's Heaven. "They rest from their labours." Yes; but that word "labours" means painful strain. In eternal, untiring youth and strength we shall be occupied in doing His blessed will in helping and blessing the wide universe that He has made. Who can tell what glorious ministrations, what infinite activities, what endless growth and progress, and lifting up of brethren, God has in store for us through all eternity. Thank God for the thought of that joyous work of never-tiring youth and vigour; work of men proudly rejoicing in their strength, helping the weak ones, teaching the ignorant aye! perhaps for the very best of us going out with Christ into the outer darkness to seek that which is lost until He find it. For even that is not shut out beyond the bounds of possibility in the impenetrable mys-

tery of the Hereafter. Do you know Whittier's
beautiful poem of the old monk who had spent
his whole life in hard and menial work for the
rescue and help of others? And when he is
dying his confessor tells him work is over,
"Thou shalt sit down and have endless prayers,
and wear a golden crown for ever and ever in
Heaven." "Ah," he says, "I'm a stupid old
man. I'm dull at prayers. I can't keep awake,
but I love my fellow men. I could be good to
the worst of them. I could not bear to sit
amongst the lazy saints and turn a deaf ear to
the sore complaints of those that suffer. I
don't want your idle Heaven. I want still to
work for others." The confessor in anger left
him, and in the night came the voice of his
Lord —

"Tender and most compassionate. Never fear,
For Heaven is love, as God Himself is love;
Thy work below shall be thy work above."[1]

Be sure that the repose of Heaven will be no
idling in flowery meadows or sitting for ever in
a big temple at worship, as the poor, weary

[1] Whittier, "The Brother of Mercy."

little children are sometimes told after a long sermon in church. No, "there is no temple in Heaven," we are told—no Church. Because all life is such a glad serving and rejoicing in God that men need no special times and places for doing it.

IV. Shall We Know One Another In Heaven?

What else can we learn? Shall we know one another? Does any one really doubt it who believes in God at all? What sort of Heaven would it be otherwise? What sort of comfort would there be if we did not know one another? Oh, this beggarly faith, that God has to put up with, that treats the Father above as it would treat a man of doubtful character. "I must have His definite texts. I must have His written pledges, else I will not believe any good thing in His dealing." That is our way. We talk very piously about our belief in God's love, but we are afraid to infer anything, to argue anything from the infinitude of that love. No, we must have God's bond signed and sealed. I do believe that one reason why we have not more of direct answers about the mysteries of the future life is because God thought that no such answer should be necessary—that His love, if one would only believe in it, is a sufficient answer to them all.

There is less need of discussing the subject here, since we have already dealt with the question of Recognition in the Intermediate Life (Part I, Chapter VII). If even in that imperfect state "absent from the body" we saw reason to hope for recognition, think how that hope rises .to certainty in the great perfect life of Heaven where "I" shall be again "in the body" the glorious perfect spiritual body.

As I have pointed out the Bible gives only passing hints on the subject. But it comforts the mourners with the thought of meeting those whom Christ will bring with Him. What would be the good of meeting if they should not know them ? St. Paul expects to meet his converts and present them before Christ. How could he do so if he did not know them ? Our Lord depicts Dives and Lazarus even in the lower Hades life as knowing each other. He says to the dying thief as they went within the veil, "To-day shalt thou be with Me." What could it mean except they should know each other within ?

But surely the Bible does not need to say it. It is one of those things that we may assume with certainty. We know that Heaven would scarce be Heaven at all if we were to be but solitary isolated spirits amongst a crowd of others whom we did not know or love. We know that the next world and this world come from the same God who is the same always. We know that in this world He has bound us up in groups, knowing and loving and sympathizing with each other. Unless His method utterly changes He must do the same hereafter. And we have seen what a prophecy of recognition lies deep in the very fibres of that nature which God has implanted in us. If we shall not know one another, why is there this undying memory of departed ones, the aching void that is never filled on earth? The lower animals lose their young and in a few days forget them. But the poor, human mother never forgets. When her head is bowed with age, when she has forgotten nearly all else on earth, you can bring the tears into her eyes by mentioning the child that died in her arms forty years ago. Did God implant that divine love in her only to disappoint it? God forbid! A thou- sand times, no. In that world the mother shall meet her child, and the lonely widow shall meet her husband, and they shall learn fully the love of God in that rapturous meeting with Christ's benediction resting on them.

I know there are further questions rising in our hearts. Will our dear ones remember us? Will they, in all the years of progress, have grown too good and great for fellowship with us? There is no specific answer save what we can infer from the boundless goodness and kindness of God. Since He does not for- get us we may be sure they will not forget us. Since His superior greatness and holiness does not put Him beyond our reach, we may be sure that theirs will not—their growth will be mainly a growth of love which will only bring them closer to us for ever and ever.

V.   How do Men Enter Heaven?

We have asked, What is meant by Heaven? What can be known of the details of life in Heaven? And now I close this book with the solemn question for us all: How shall we enter

Heaven? If you have followed me thus far
the answer is easy. Though there is a special
place which shall be Heaven, yet, if Heaven
means a state of mind rather than a place of
residence, if Heaven means to be something
rather than to go somewhere, though it means
to go somewhere, too, then the answer is easy.
We enter Heaven by a spiritual, not by a natural act. We begin Heaven here on earth,
not by taking a journey to the sun or the
planets, not by taking a journey from this
world up through the air, but by taking a journey from a bad state of mind to a good state
of mind; from that state of mind which is en-
mity against God, to that of humble, loyal,
loving obedience to Christ. It is not so much
that we have to go to Heaven. We have to do
that, too. But Heaven has to come to us first.
Heaven has to begin in ourselves. "The beginning of Heaven is not at that hour when
the eye grows dim and the sound of friendly
voices becomes silent in death, but at that hour
when God draws near and the eyes of the spiritual understanding are opened, and the soul
sees how beautiful Christ is, how hateful sin
is; the hour when self-will is crucified, and

the God-will is born in the resolutions of a new heart." Then Heaven has begun, the Heaven that will continue after our death.

Do we believe that this is the right way to think of Heaven? For if so it is a serious question for us all. What about my hopes of entering Heaven? If Heaven consists of character rather than possessions, of a state of mind rather than a place of residence, if, in fine, Heaven has to begin on earth, what of our hopes of entering Heaven? Is it not pitiful to hear people talk lightly about going to Heaven, whose lives on earth have not any trace of the love and purity and nobleness and self-sacrifice of which Heaven shall entirely consist hereafter? To see men with the carnal notions about Heaven as a place of external glory and beauty and jasper and emerald, where, after they have misused their time on earth, they shall fly away like swallows to an eternal summer. Why, what should they do in Heaven? They would be miserable there even if they could get there. They would be entirely out of their element, like a fish sent to live on the grass of a lovely meadow. Those who shall enjoy the Heaven hereafter are they whose Heaven has begun before. They who may hope to do the work of God hereafter are those who are humbly trying to do that will on earth. These shall inherit the everlasting Kingdom. Unto which blessed Kingdom may He vouchsafe to bring us all! Amen.

Printed in the United States of America

Printed in the United Kingdom
by Lightning Source UK Ltd.
115475UKS00001B/167